DILEMMAS OF BRAZILIAN GRAND STRATEGY

INTRODUCTION

Only a few years after America's post-September 11, 2001 (9/11) displays of military might led commentators like Charles Krauthammer to opine that the post-Cold War "unipolar moment" was on the verge of becoming a prolonged "unipolar era," the international system seems to be moving toward a more diffuse distribution of power. The United States is widely (if perhaps debatably) assumed to be in relative decline; a range of second- and third-tier powers are jockeying for greater influence. It is now common to hear that the world is moving toward a "post-American" age, that we have reached the "end of American exceptionalism" or "the end of American hegemony"—the common themes in these assessments being the ebbing of U.S. supremacy and the rise of a new class of powers that will rival Washington for influence in the 21st century.[1]

Few countries have experienced as remarkable an improvement in their international stature over the past decade as Brazil. Brazil has long had a reputation as a country with a great future—if only it could get there. As late as 2002, Brazil was wrestling with chronic financial instability, and the election of a president with a distinguished leftist heritage raised fears of macroeconomic collapse and resurgent political strife. Since then, however, Brazilian President Luiz Inácio Lula da Silva has won widespread praise for his economic and social initiatives. Building on the initiatives of his predecessor, Brazilian President Fernando Henrique Cardoso, President Lula has sought to channel the growing national confidence derived from democratic consolidation and macroeconomic stability into a more forceful diplomacy. Brazil has become more active in United Nations (UN) peacekeeping missions; it has energetically promoted the India, Brazil, and South Africa (IBSA), and Brazil, Russia, India, and China (BRIC) forums as alternative centers of global power; it has forged economic and technological partnerships with France, Russia, China, and other key countries; it has put forward a claim to a permanent seat on the UN Security Council; and it has promoted South American economic integration as well as new regional institutions like the Union of South American Nations (UNASUR) and the South American Defense Council (CSD). Underlying all this is a sense among Brazilian policymakers that their country has finally arrived on the global scene, and that it is destined to reap the benefits of the ongoing changes in the international system. In this spirit, President Lula has announced that Brazil will become a great power in this century, and Brazilian official discourse is infused with a sense of national strength and purpose. "Brazil must think big," said Defense Minister Nelson Jobim in 2009. "This is the moment in which it's necessary to be audacious in order to advance. . . . There is no longer any possibility of asking Brazil, on the international stage, to take positions that run contrary to its interests."[2]

Purely by dint of its size and economic capacity, Brazil will exert a strong pull on regional and global politics in the coming decades. Even under the most optimistic projections, however, Brazil will not possess the economic or military capacity to compete with other major powers—namely the United States, China, and the European Union (EU)—for decades, if then. If Brazil is to achieve what political scientists call "systemic impact" — the ability to shape the global order in meaningful ways — it will have to do so not through the inexorable accumulation of geopolitical weight, but through the resourcefulness of its strategy and diplomacy. Accordingly, this monograph examines Brazilian grand strategy as it has developed under President Lula with an eye to illuminating its characteristics, prospects, and implications for the international system in general and the United States in particular. The present is a propitious time for such an undertaking; with President Lula set to leave office at the end of 2010, Brazilian grand strategy may be approaching an inflection point, making a proper understanding of the strategy pursued over the last 8 years all the more important for Brazilian and U.S. observers alike.[3]

This monograph makes two principal arguments, one pertaining to the nature of Brazilian grand strategy, the second regarding its ramifications and chances for success. Under President Lula, Brazil has followed a multi-layered grand strategy that emphasizes a gradual and peaceful — yet nonetheless significant — revision of the international order. While Brazilian officials recognize the benefits that their nation has derived from the *Pax Americana,* they still view the current order — characterized by U.S. military and strategic hegemony and the economic hegemony of the West — as prejudicial to the development, commercial interests, and diplomatic influence of emerging countries like Brazil. The fundamental goal of Brazilian grand strategy has thus been to hasten the transition from the dominance of the developed world to a multipolar order in which international power balances and institutions are more favorable to the assertion of Brazil's interests. Because Brazil still faces, and will continue to face, a relative deficit of economic and military might, President Lula has resorted to a strategy commonly used by "middle powers," countries that rely on multilateralism, coalition-building, and other such methods to achieve systemic influence. At the global level, he has sought to strengthen international norms and organizations that can check American power, a classic soft-balancing technique. He has also forged overlapping webs of bilateral partnerships and multilateral coalitions designed to diversify Brazil's commerce, improve its strategic flexibility, and augment its leverage in international negotiations. This has entailed embracing players from the entire spectrum of international actors, including countries — Iran being one notable example — that are deeply hostile to the United States. At the regional level, President Lula has committed himself to establishing Brazil as the recognized leader of a more united South America, with the aim of expanding his country's power base and hitching its global ambitions to the aggregate geopolitical weight of its continent.

This grand strategy has clearly benefited Brazil in the short term, raising the country's international profile and creating an array of strategic, commercial, and diplomatic options that President Lula's successors may pursue.[4] Yet Brazilian grand strategy also entails four key dilemmas that President Lula has not been able to resolve, which could obstruct or at the very least complicate the country's geopolitical ascent. First, issues like poor infrastructure, rampant crime, and excessive taxation and regulation of the economy may impede Brazil from attaining the strong economic growth and social cohesion necessary to sustain such an audacious strategic project. Second, in dealing with South America, the Brazilian political class has not reconciled its desire for regional leadership with its unwillingness to share power or economic benefits with its neighbors. As a result, many of these countries perceive Brazil's diplomacy to be domineering and its trade policies to be narrowly self-interested, and they have thus refused to support President Lula's bid for regional preeminence. Third, at the global level, the long-term usefulness of President Lula's various "strategic partnerships" and alliances is open to question. The IBSA and BRIC forums are much less cohesive—and thus less diplomatically effective—than they appear at first glance, and pursuing close relationships with countries like Iran may ultimately hurt Brazil's democratic image and create more problems than opportunities. Fourth, while President Lula has maintained good relations with Washington, his grand strategy unavoidably entails a growing risk of conflict over issues like Iran, trade policy, and the U.S. diplomatic and military role in Latin America. If not managed carefully, these frictions could eventually push U.S.-Brazil relations in a tenser, less productive direction, impairing the interests of both countries. Looking ahead, the efficacy of Brazilian grand strategy—and its consequences for U.S. interests—will be contingent on how President Lula's successors address these dilemmas.

The remainder of this monograph consists of four sections. The first discusses Brazil's strategic culture, the issues that have traditionally frustrated its desires for global influence, and the factors underlying the growing assertiveness of its foreign policy since the return to democratic rule in 1985. The second describes President Lula's worldview and details the military, diplomatic, and commercial components of his grand strategy. The third evaluates this grand strategy, noting its accomplishments but also emphasizing the four key dilemmas mentioned above. The fourth discusses implications for U.S. and Brazilian policymakers and offers some brief concluding remarks.

BRAZILIAN STRATEGIC CULTURE AND THE QUEST FOR GREATNESS

When President Lula proclaimed in 2003 that Brazil was ready to "assume its greatness," he expressed a deeply held tenet of Brazilian national ideology and strategic culture. Since the formation of the Republic in 1889, a variety of factors—Brazil's continental dimensions, its commanding economic and strategic position within South America, its relative lack of territorial threats, and its sense of exceptionalism within the Latin American context—have inspired a belief that the country belongs among the global elite. "We possess all the conditions that enable us to aspire to a place among the world's great powers," said Carlos de Meira Mattos, the Deputy Chief of Staff of the Armed Forces, during the 1970s.[5]

This belief was at the core of Brazilian diplomacy for much of the 20th century. During World War II, Brazil was the only Latin American country to contribute ground forces to the Allied cause, deploying an entire division to Italy. Following the coup against João Goulart in 1964, the military governments that ruled for the next 21 years touted the notion of *O Brasil Grande* (Greater Brazil). The ideological underpinnings of authoritarian rule—a collection of concepts developed at the *Escola Superior de Guerra* and known as National Security Doctrine—emphasized geopolitical thinking and the projection of national power. These administrations pursued a firmly anti-communist foreign policy within South America, but simultaneously sought to expand Brazilian influence in Lusophone Africa and the Third World and thereby break out of the bipolar framework dominated by the superpowers. Brazil, announced Foreign Minister Antônio Azeredo da Silveira in 1975, must achieve "an outstanding position in the world," free from "the paths of hegemonic construction of the past."[6] Prominent international observers shared this high opinion of Brazil's potential. Henry Kissinger privately predicted that "in 50 years Brazil should have achieved world power status," and George Kennan labeled Brazil one of several "monster countries" that might exert a decisive influence on the global scene.[7]

Until recently, however, ambition continually outpaced reality. Brazil's regional rivalry with Argentina and its condescending attitude toward its neighbors prevented it from establishing a strong power base within its home continent (and these two factors continue to loom as obstacles to Brazilian strategy today). Political instability absorbed the attention of the Brazilian elite; authoritarian rule between 1964 and 1985 drained Brazilian credibility abroad. Under the military governments that ruled during this period, Brazil was something of a pariah state, as these regimes' human rights violations and refusal to renounce nuclear weapons left the country isolated in international forums. Recurring economic crises, most notably the hyperinflation and massive debt burdens of the 1980s and 1990s, further sapped Brazilian strategic potential. These difficulties often made Brazil seem more like a basket case than a rising power, and in some international economic circles, there remains skepticism as to the country's long-term trajectory.[8]

Over the past 20 years, however, Brazil has steadily increased its international role, first under three democratic presidents in the 1990s, and then more rapidly under President Lula since 2003. In one sense, this activism was born of necessity. As Brazil opened its economy during the 1980s and 1990s, it became more sensitive to patterns of globalization forged by the leading developed countries and institutions like the World Trade Organization (WTO) and the General Agreement on Tariffs and Trade (GATT). As a result, the only way to protect Brazilian interests and promote Brazilian development was to take a more active part in shaping the norms, rules, and organizations that governed the global economy and international relations more broadly. As President Fernando Henrique Cardoso (1995-2002) put it, the policy of "autonomy through distance" pursued by the military dictatorships must be replaced by one of "autonomy through participation, within a changing international reality."[9] Brazil took a more participatory attitude toward numerous international institutions, contributed to several peacekeeping missions under UN mandate, and led the formation of regional groupings like Mercosul (Common Market of the South) as a way of increasing its bargaining power in international economic negotiations.[10]

What has enabled and sustained these initiatives is Brazil's relatively high degree of recent economic and political progress. The consolidation of a stable, multiparty democracy has calmed the political vicissitudes that previously intruded upon foreign policy and has given Brazilian leaders greater credibility in interacting with a world where democratic rule has advanced dramatically since the 1970s. In the same vein, the fact that Brazil has restored macroeconomic equilibrium and made gradual progress in addressing widespread poverty through conditional cash transfer

(CCT) programs like *Bolsa Familia* has permitted its diplomats to take a more vocal role in global debates on poverty and development. As Marco Aurélio Garcia, one of President Lula's chief advisers on foreign affairs, acknowledges, "Without the successes of his social policy, President Lula would not be as respected internationally."[11]

Moreover, while macroeconomic growth has been anemic in recent decades, factors like improved economic stability, growing purchasing power for the poor and middle class, and the development of both internal and external markets have allowed Brazil to crack the top 10 in rankings of the world's largest economies (as measured in gross domestic product [GDP] at purchasing power parity).[12] Prominent commentators, including Goldman Sachs, predict that the country may climb as high as fifth in this ranking in the next 40 years.[13] A thriving biofuels program combined with aggressive offshore drilling has addressed Brazil's internal fuel needs and increased its international economic influence amid concerns about the long-term cost and availability of petroleum supplies, and the exploitation of the offshore Tupi oil field will likely make Brazil a major player in the hydrocarbon market.[14] These developments have not only increased Brazilian economic power and diplomatic standing; they have also raised national self-confidence after the trials of the 1980s and 1990s and allowed the foreign policy community to argue that progress at home justifies and requires expanded ambitions abroad. President Lula alluded to this dynamic when he declared that "Brazil is ready, Brazil is mature, Brazil is aware of the game which has to be played."[15] Understanding how President Lula has played this game requires a closer examination of his worldview.

GRAND STRATEGY UNDER PRESIDENT LULA

Brazilian grand strategy under President Lula has been rooted in a deeply ambivalent view of the international system. In one sense, Brazil has benefited enormously from "public goods" that the United States and its Western partners provided during the postwar—and now the post-Cold War—era. The liberalization of global economic and financial flows has been a boon to Brazilian development, especially as that country has opened its own economy over the past 2 decades. For all of Brazil's complaints about the International Monetary Fund (IMF) and the World Bank, these institutions have provided development assistance and a financial safety net of which Brazil has more than once availed itself. The long-standing U.S. defense umbrella over the Western Hemisphere has afforded Brazil a degree of free security from external threat. Similarly, Washington's policing of the global commons has allowed Brazil to trade around the world without building a Navy capable of protecting that commerce. In this sense, Brazil is very much a "winner" in the *Pax Americana*.[16]

Nonetheless, the prevailing global order still strikes many Brazilians as fundamentally inequitable. The UN Security Council is controlled by the five permanent members (P-5), even though this arrangement distorts current geopolitical realities and keeps latecomers like Brazil, India, and Japan from rising to the top echelon of international politics. "The geography of 2009 is different from the geography of 1948 when the UN was created," President Lula has pointedly noted.[17] The unipolarity of the current system is also troubling. There is no meaningful counterweight to the "unilateral" exercise of American power, a fact that became quite clear in the run-up to the Iraq war. These issues inform a strong undercurrent of anxiety in Brazilian geopolitical analysis. "We live in a world in which intimidation threatens to trample common sense underfoot," said Strategic Affairs Minister Roberto Mangabeira in 2008.[18]

International trade and financial arrangements appear similarly ossified from a Brazilian perspective. Because organizations like the IMF, World Bank, and WTO are still dominated by the developed Western countries, Brazilian officials frequently complain that the policies of these institutions are slanted against the interests of the developing world. This impression has been reinforced by the persistence of U.S. and European agricultural subsidies that inhibit the export of Brazilian commodities. These subsidies, President Lula argued at the UN General Assembly in 2006, "are oppressive shackles that hold back progress and doom poor countries to backwardness."[19] President Lula particularly objects to the 54-cent per gallon U.S. tariff on ethanol imports, and since 2003, Brazil has refused to allow the Doha Round of the WTO negotiations to proceed until its concerns on agricultural subsidies are addressed.[20] Brazilian discomfort with prevailing international economic structures became starkly evident in a series of comments made by top-level officials in 2008 and 2009. Foreign Minister Celso Amorim compared U.S. trade representatives to Nazi propagandists, and President Lula asserted that the world financial crisis was caused by "the irrational behavior of white people with blue eyes."[21]

Brazilian strategic analysis thus features a pervasive sense of danger—a fear that the strictures of the current global order might impede Brazil's development or otherwise limit its potential. But it is also characterized by a sense of opportunity. Brazilian officials acknowledge that the United States remains the dominant player in the international system, but they view it as unlikely that Washington can maintain this position indefinitely. As early as the 1990s, a high-ranking official in the Defense Ministry commented on "the visible imbalance between its military hegemony and its worrying economic situation, with its huge domestic and external debt and the technological and administrative competition from other world powers."[22] Since then, other officials have openly opined that the United States is in relative decline. As American power ebbs, the global system will gradually approach a point of greater geopolitical flexibility, an opening that rising nations like Brazil can exploit to attain greater influence and freedom of maneuver. "If we know how to work in the 21st century," said President Lula early in his presidency, "this will be the century of the so-called emerging countries, like India, Brazil, South Africa, China, Mexico, and Russia, hitherto considered second-class nations."[23]

Under President Lula, the chief aim of Brazilian grand strategy has been to work for what Minister Amorim calls "a certain reconfiguration of the world's commercial and diplomatic geography"—that is, to hasten the transition to a multipolar order in which international norms and institutions no longer favor the developed world at Brazil's expense.[24] Along these lines, President Lula has defined Brazilian foreign policy as an "assertive" project rather than a "subaltern" stance that would imply "acceptance of the guidelines set by the big power blocs, the U.S. and Europe."[25] In a speech in September 2003, President Lula outlined this diplomatic philosophy in dramatic terms:

12

We no longer accept participation in international politics as if we were Latin American wretches; a Third World country of no account; a worthless country with homeless children; a minor country whose people only know how to play soccer and dance the samba. . . . There is no interlocutor anywhere in the world who respects another who bows his head and acts as an inferior.[26]

During his time in office, President Lula has pursued a multi-layered strategy for asserting Brazilian interests and increasing its global power.

Hard Power and Military Capabilities.

One element of this strategy involves accumulating traditional hard-power capabilities. "Realists" such as John Mearsheimer predict that rising powers will seek to increase their influence and challenge the global hegemon by amassing greater military might, and President Lula has indeed laid much stress on strengthening Brazil's armed forces.[27] Military spending increased from $9.23 billion to $23.9 billion between 2003 and 2009, permitting major technological upgrades.[28] Brazil has purchased attack helicopters from France and Russia, combat aircraft and military transports from European suppliers, as well as four French-made *Scorpene* submarines. There are also plans to develop a nuclear attack submarine in cooperation with France, and Brazilian officials have arranged to purchase or develop short-range missiles, night vision equipment, and thermal and electronic sensors.[29] Beyond all this, the government has presided over the completion and deployment of the Amazon Surveillance System (SIVAM), an extensive network of satellites, ground sensors, and radars that can monitor not only Brazil's vast Amazonian hinterland but also parts of Colombia, Venezuela, Bolivia, Guyana, Suriname, and other neighboring countries.[30]

Brazil is not simply purchasing equipment; it is also negotiating agreements that will allow it to develop its military-industrial base and eventually eliminate any dependence on foreign suppliers. "We are not engaging in a shopping festival," says Minister Jobim, "but in a festival of national technical improvement based on the transfer of technology." Brazilian representatives have emphasized joint partnerships between Brazilian firms and their foreign counterparts and told European suppliers that they are only interested in purchases that involve no-strings-attached technology transfers. Given the eagerness of European suppliers to satisfy Brazil's appetite for advanced weaponry, it has not been difficult to negotiate a range of joint projects that will result in the construction of fighter aircraft, attack helicopters, and, perhaps most notably, the aforementioned nuclear submarine.[31]

These acquisitions are part of a broader shift in Brazilian military strategy and doctrine. Brazil is moving away from its traditional defense posture, in which the majority of its forces were deployed in the southern part of the country, to a newer stance that focuses on securing internal portions of the country from criminal urban guerrillas and protecting conflict-prone border regions in the Amazon. This latter goal derives from not simply the need to avert instability along Brazil's frontiers, but also an exaggerated fear that foreign powers, particularly the United States, covet geopolitical space and natural resources in the Brazilian Amazon. Along the same lines, defense officials have broached the possibility of patrolling the

South Atlantic and called for measures to protect the country's offshore hydrocarbon resources.[32] There are also plans to develop an asymmetric warfare capability geared toward frustrating attacks by larger powers, as well as a greater emphasis on rapid national mobilization in crises. Brazil's armed forces, one planning document states, must be organized "around a military culture hallmarked by flexibility, imagination, and daring, [with] the capacity to surprise and overwhelm."[33]

President Lula's military policy is meant to serve multiple purposes, several of which have more to do with domestic politics than global ambitions. At the level of national strategy, however, this buildup is clearly linked to the drive for greater autonomy and influence. In planning documents and comments by high-ranking officials, the nation's growing military capabilities are frequently characterized as a means of shaping events in Brazil's neighborhood and a "defense shield" against meddling by hegemonic powers. Just as important, the buildup serves as a symbol of growing national power and a signal to both regional and global observers that Brazil intends to pursue a serious geostrategic role. In 2008, the Chief of Staff of Brazil's Navy told an interviewer, "Those who have nuclear submarines sit on the United Nations Security Council. All permanent members have the technology, which none of them give up. We have to develop our own."[34] In this same spirit, Brazil has participated in numerous UN peacekeeping missions since the 1990s, and President Lula's government eagerly took the lead in commanding the UN stabilization mission deployed to Haiti in 2004. As Minister Jobim explained in 2008, "What we want is to have voice and vote in the international arena, and this only goes to countries that have a defense structure to deter and to express national power."[35]

President Lula has clearly not neglected the military foundations of international influence. Even so, Brazilian officials do not perceive grand strategy primarily in hard-power terms. Military spending as a percentage of GDP still lags compared to many countries in South America, and even with recent technological upgrades, Brazil will not be able to project significant military power outside its immediate environs for decades, if then.[36] In a broader strategic sense, American military and technological superiority is so pronounced that even if Brazil desired to compete militarily with the United States (and there is little indication it does), any attempt to do so would be futile and counterproductive. Nor will this power deficit change anytime soon. Military power is ultimately derived from economic power, and even the most optimistic forecasts of Brazilian growth over the next 40 years still place that country far behind other centers of global economic power like the United States, China, and the EU.[37] If Brazilian foreign policy is to satisfy President Lula's grand ambitions, military capabilities will have relatively little to do with it.

Middle Power Strategies: Soft Balancing, Coalition-Building, and Region Formation.

This challenge is a common one for middle powers. According to international relations theorists like Robert Keohane, middle powers are states that reside on the periphery of the global elite. They frequently harbor great-power ambitions and may exert significant influence within a certain area or region, but they lack the material capabilities to confront the hege-

16

monic power (or powers) or to play a central role in shaping the international system. For middle powers, achieving global influence thus necessitates punching above their own weight, generally through astute multilateral diplomacy. A middle power might forge diplomatic alliances with other rising nations as a way of magnifying its own influence; it might use international norms and organizations to restrain the behavior of the hegemonic power; it might seek to establish itself as the leader of a distinct geographic region and thereby harness its ambitions to the combined geopolitical weight of its neighbors. As Keohane writes, middle powers "cannot act alone effectively, but may be able to have a systemic impact in a small group or through an international institution."[38] In short, a "middle power strategy" is effectively one of coalition-building and soft balancing.[39]

Brazilian officials are keenly aware of their status as a middle power—as well as the strategic imperatives that flow from that status. Samuel Pinheiro Guimarães, Secretary General of the Ministry of External Relations (*Ministério das Relações Exteriores,* or Itamaraty) under President Lula, argued that "Brazil has to articulate political, economic, and technological alliances with peripheral states of the international system to defend and protect its interests."[40] Such a strategy plays to Brazil's strengths. Itamaraty is the best diplomatic service in Latin America, and its representatives receive rigorous professional and linguistic training. (In recognition of this strength, President Lula's government decided to expand Itamaraty by several hundred diplomats in 2006.) Efforts at multilateral coordination are also facilitated by President Lula's charisma and his credibility—especially among the developing countries—in addressing issues like poverty and governance. At the broadest, systemic level, a middle-power strategy naturally appeals to other nations that are uncomfortable with some aspect of American hegemony.[41]

During President Lula's presidency, Brazilian diplomacy has featured at least three pronounced characteristics of a middle-power grand strategy. The first of these involves fortifying international norms and institutions that can act as a brake on American power. Conscious that U.S. negotiating power is diluted when Washington has to deal with its trading partners through international forums rather than bilateral settings, Brazilian officials have placed great importance on broadening the basis of world trade and financial negotiations. President Lula has diligently lobbied for the G-8 to be replaced by the G-20, a larger group that includes emerging countries like China, Brazil, India, and Mexico. Similarly, his government has relied on WTO rules and procedures to restrain what it views as unfair trade behavior by the United States and other developed countries, and Brazil has increasingly looked to this organization as a forum for articulating its economic interests vis-à-vis the West. This has taken the form of positive action, as when President Lula's representatives led the charge for concessions on the licensing of AIDS drugs, but it has also taken the form of obstruction, as when Brazil used the WTO framework to rally opposition to Western agricultural subsidies and block the Doha Round negotiations. "The strengthening of the multilateral trading system is essential to those with less political and economic leverage," Minister Amorim explained in 2007.[42]

This same approach has governed President Lula's views on the UN and the use of force. Alarmed by recent instances of "unilateral" U.S. military action,

Brazilian officials have responded by seeking to deny international legitimacy to such endeavors. In March 2003, President Lula spoke out strongly against the impending U.S. invasion of Iraq, saying that it "disrespects the United Nations" and "doesn't take into account what the rest of the world thinks."[43] Since then, a central rhetorical trope of Brazilian diplomacy has been a dogged insistence that the unilateral offensive use of force is inherently illegitimate, and that military intervention is warranted only when carried out under the sanction of international institutions like the Security Council. "We reject the view of an international order which favors the use of force and regards multilateralism as just one among many options on the menu, to be selected when it suits the objectives of the powerful," says Minister Amorim.[44] The Brazilian government has lent substance to this discourse by voting against the U.S. invasion of Iraq in 2003, while also participating in Security Council-sponsored peacekeeping missions in East Timor, Haiti, and elsewhere. President Lula has frequently used bilateral and multilateral communiqués to call for a revitalization of the Council's collective security functions.[45] All this indicates a classic soft-balancing technique, one meant to set a high threshold for the legitimacy of U.S. military action and thereby raise the diplomatic costs should Washington decide to employ its overwhelming military might.

A close corollary to this effort has been President Lula's bid to win Brazil a permanent seat on the Security Council. This desire owes mainly to hardheaded calculations of national prestige and influence; a permanent seat would serve as a symbol of Brazil's arrival on the global stage and permit it to shape debates on international diplomacy and the use of force. Even so, President Lula has shrewdly framed this quest as part of a broader, more altruistic campaign to make the international order more consensual and its governing bodies more representative. The need, he said in 2009, is "to build a new international order that is sustainable, multilateral and less asymmetric, free of hegemonies and ruled by democratic institutions." Along these lines, Brazil has played a key role in coordinating the activities of the G-4, an arrangement in which Brazil, India, Japan, and Germany have agreed to support one another's bids for permanent seats on the Security Council.[46]

President Lula's reliance on the G-4 as the vehicle for his Security Council ambitions indicates a second aspect of Brazil's middle-power strategy. This aspect involves building coalitions that offset the diplomatic and economic asymmetries of a unipolar system and serve as force-multipliers for Brazilian influence. President Lula has cultivated "strategic partnerships" with a wide range of countries, including developed middle-powers like Russia and France, as a means to this end. Yet the foremost emphasis of his coalition-building strategy has been on expanding cooperation with other "Southern," or developing countries.[47] According to President Lula and his top advisers— namely Minister Amorim, Marco Aurélio Garcia, and Guimarães—the strategic interests of Brazil and other major developing countries are fundamentally convergent. Because Brazil is geographically removed from countries like China and India, it need not fear them as rivals; because these nations share Brazil's interest in replacing unipolarity with a more flexible international order, they might well be its natural diplomatic partners. "Despite the differences between Brazil and other large peripheral states," Guimarães argued in 1999, "inasmuch as they share common characteristics and interests and are far away from one another, they do not have direct competitive interests and are therefore able to construct common political projects."[48] If Brazil can give impetus to these projects, it can increase its geopolitical leverage and position itself as the voice of the Third World in its dealings with the West.

The imperative of "South-South" cooperation has given rise to a wide array of bilateral and multilateral initiatives. On the bilateral front, President Lula has been more attentive than any of his predecessors to the potential benefits of a closer relationship with China, which could eventually serve as the core of an extremely powerful Southern diplomatic or economic bloc. Trade with China increased 12-fold between 2001 and 2009, making that country Brazil's largest commercial partner, and Brazil will become a major source of oil for Beijing once the Tupi field reaches full production. There is also a growing degree of technological and military cooperation between the two countries, which complements the deals that President Lula has struck with Russia and France.[49]

A more controversial bilateral initiative is President Lula's vocal support for the Islamic regime in Iran. President Lula welcomed Iranian President Mahmoud Ahmadinejad to Brazil only a few months after the allegedly fraudulent June 2009 elections in Iran, and he has pointedly refused to condemn Iran's nuclear program or support a move toward UN sanctions. In May 2010, President Lula joined with Turkish diplomats in brokering a nuclear agreement that would allow Tehran to ship only a portion of its uranium abroad for enrichment, a move widely seen as an effort to help Iran avoid the imposition of a new round of sanctions by the Security Council. While this stance has occasioned criticism from Brazilian conservatives and U.S. observers, President Lula appears to see good relations with Tehran as a way of asserting Brazil's autonomy vis-à-vis Washington, making itself a player in Middle Eastern politics, and potentially positioning itself as a mediator between Iran and the West—all of which fit nicely with Brazil's broader middle power strategy. As Minister Amorim puts it, Iran is "the new geographic partner in our country's policy."[50]

With respect to multilateral arrangements, President Lula's focus on South-South diplomacy first captured global attention at the Cancun summit, part of the Doha Round of WTO talks, in late 2003. When the United States and the EU pressured the developing countries to accept the "Singapore Package" (a raft of measures pertaining to investment, competition, trade, and transparency in government procurement, which together constituted the core of the Doha agenda), President Lula seized the opportunity to organize a Third-World revolt. Brazil led more than 20 developing countries in demanding that any progress on the Singapore Package be accompanied by a rollback of agricultural subsidies in the United States and Europe. Taking this position lent political cover to the smaller members of the group, and after U.S. efforts to break this front failed, the meeting ended without agreement. More than that, the stalemate created by Brazil's opposition led to the breakdown of the Doha Round, with the major participants unable to agree even on a framework for continuing the negotiations. (Discussions eventually resumed a year later, but the core dispute underscored by the failure of the Cancun summit has not yet been resolved.) This deadlock hardly benefited Brazil economically and it effectively stymied the world trade agenda, but it raised President Lula's global profile and allowed him to act as a champion of developing-country interests in subsequent trade meetings. Afterward, President Lula and his advisers regularly referred to the Cancun summit as a watershed in Brazilian diplomacy. "The world saw that Brazil was able to say no," Minister Amorim later recalled.[51]

Since 2003, Brazilian officials have worked to formalize South-South cooperation through several overlapping initiatives. While the BRIC forum is not technically a club of developing countries due to Russia's inclusion, it embodies the peripheral-state ethos at the heart of Brazilian grand strategy. President Lula and Minister Amorim have stated on numerous occasions that they view BRIC as an emerging trade bloc that will eventually constitute an alternative to the Western-dominated system led by the United States and the EU, and bilateral commerce between Brazil and the other members has risen dramatically over the past several years. Making BRIC a more formal partnership is central to increasing its internal cohesion and overall geopolitical weight, and Brazilian officials have played a key role in establishing regular ministerial meetings, summits, and working group discussions.[52]

For all the attention BRIC has received, the IBSA Dialogue Forum may be the most important piece of Brazil's South-South diplomacy. Founded by Brazilian initiative in 2003, IBSA represents an explicit attempt, as one communiqué put it, to "amplify the collective voice of the South."[53] The group includes three of the largest democracies in the developing world, boasting a combined population of over 1.4 billion and an aggregate GDP of over $3 trillion, and its leaders have laid out an audacious program for strengthening IBSA and increasing its international reach.[54] IBSA aims to increase trilateral trade within the group to $25 billion by 2015 and it has established nearly 20 working groups on everything from commerce and investment to the environment.[55] The forum sponsors development projects in Guinea-Bissau and Haiti as a form of outreach to poorer Third-World countries, and in 2008 a joint naval exercise raised the prospect of an eventual IBSA military capability. "I don't think that a group of sociologists meeting in a room causes such attention," said Minister Amorim, "but a group of boats assembling with their flags causes attention."[56] The members have also pledged to support one another's Security Council ambitions and advanced common positions on issues like nonproliferation and nuclear energy. Brazilian officials argue that IBSA carries extra legitimacy because its members are all developing, multicultural democracies, and comments by President Lula and Minister Amorim leave no doubt that they view the group as an emerging axis of geopolitical and economic power. IBSA, said Minister Amorim in 2007, is one of the tools that "can improve our negotiating capacity and help build a multi-polar world."[57]

The third element of Brazil's grand strategy takes place at the regional rather than the global level. According to international relations theorists, middle powers may augment their influence through a process known as "region formation," whereby they simultaneously define their region as a distinct geopolitical entity and claim leadership status within that entity. Doing so allows the middle power to act as an acknowledged regional leader in global forums, thereby improving its diplomatic credibility and negotiating capacity.[58] If region formation leads to meaningful economic or political integration, it can bring about the pooling of resources and a corresponding increase in the aggregate geopolitical strength of both the region and its leading power. This was the strategy followed by Charles de Gaulle when he sought to make France the leader of a united, independent Europe, and the same spirit has animated European integration schemes since the early Cold War. Under President Cardoso, and more so under President Lula, Brazil has followed this same general template. Brazilian officials have spoken of creating a "solid regional space" in South America, and Marco Aurélio Garcia has advanced the notion that the continent must become an autonomous power center—presumably under Brasilia's leadership. "We are marching toward a multipolar world," he said in 2009, "and South America will be one of those poles."[59]

The imperative of asserting Brazilian leadership has become all the more important in view of the contested geopolitical environment in South America. Recent U.S. policy toward Latin America has arguably been one of benign neglect, but Washington has nonetheless signed free trade agreements and strengthened relations with key countries like Chile, Colombia, and Peru. More pressing still is the issue of Venezuela, which under President Hugo Chávez has staked its own claim to regional leadership. Through projects like PetroCaribe and the Bolivarian Alliance for the Americas (ALBA, formerly the Bolivarian Alternative for the Americas), extensive aid to populist politicians in other countries, and the acquisition of advanced weapons systems from Russia and other suppliers, President Chávez has shown that he intends to make Venezuela the dominant power in South America. In public, Brazilian officials insist that they do not view President Chávez as a threat, but in private, they seem to recognize that his bid for regional leadership places Brazil in a difficult position. Openly confronting President Chávez would polarize the ideological and diplomatic climate in South America, destroying any chance for a more unified — and thus more influential — region. Yet taking too passive a stance risks allowing President Chávez to accumulate influence and isolate Brazil.[60]

Brazil has therefore taken an indirect approach to containing President Chávez. In public, President Lula has placated the Venezuelan leader and sought to mediate his disputes with Colombia's Álvaro Uribe and other conservative leaders. More quietly, Brazil has attempted to consolidate its position in the region by strengthening ties with a range of countries, including those that make up President Chávez's core diplomatic constituency. President Lula has called for a "strategic partnership" with Argentina, a long-standing rival that has traditionally viewed Brazilian influence with suspicion. Likewise, his government has expanded counternarcotics assistance to Bolivia, donated decommissioned airplanes or helicopters to Paraguay, Bolivia, and Ecuador, and used a SIVAM surveillance aircraft to help Peru resolve a hostage crisis in 2003. As part of an initiative begun prior to President Lula's presidency, Brazil has also made a virtue of its reliance on natural gas imports. Brazil co-sponsored construction of a gas pipeline running from Bolivia to Brazil, ensuring that the Bolivian gas industry has become dependent on the Brazilian market, and President Lula acquiesced in the nationalization of Brazilian-owned gas assets in Bolivia in 2006. The list of initiatives goes on; efforts to balance President Chávez and expand Brazilian influence have given President Lula's regional policy a hyperactive quality.[61]

As this diplomacy indicates, Brazil is aiming for what one scholar calls "consensual hegemony."[62] Brazilian officials seek to portray their country's diplomacy as a benign, unthreatening project so as to avoid reviving traditional fears of a hegemonic Brazil and thereby driving South American countries toward Caracas or Washington. (How successful they have been in doing so is open to dispute.) Accordingly, for Brazil to achieve effective regional leadership, it will have to forge consensual arrangements that provide its neighbors with economic and political benefits while drawing them deeper into the Brazilian orbit.

This strategy has driven the central thrust of Brazilian regional diplomacy under President Lula—his unceasing emphasis on South American integration. Regional integration is the keystone of consensual hegemony—forging deeper political and economic ties with South American countries will create a more powerful continental bloc, while binding these nations more closely to the most powerful member of that bloc. Early in his presidency, President Lula called regional integration "a strategic option to strengthen the insertion of our countries in the world, increasing their negotiating capacity," and Brazilian officials have frequently invoked the EU as an example of what they aim to accomplish.[63]

The centerpiece of this effort has traditionally been Mercosul, the trade and customs pact originally established with Argentina, Uruguay, and Paraguay 2 decades ago. When President Lula came to power, he said that fortifying Mercosul would be a top priority. Since then, his government has broached various options for deepening economic ties within the pact and called for broadening its membership and responsibilities. Mercosul now has working groups to deal with

27

organized crime, terrorism, and other security issues; it has taken on observers (Mexico) and associate members (Bolivia, Chile, Colombia, Ecuador, and Peru); and Venezuela was granted full membership in 2006 (pending approval by the Paraguayan and Brazilian legislatures). This latter decision was highly controversial, but President Lula's government deemed it necessary to increase the share of South American trade commanded by the agreement, harness the influence provided by Venezuelan oil reserves, and hopefully moderate President Chávez's efforts to undercut Brazilian diplomacy. President Lula has high hopes for Mercosul; he has pushed for a free trade agreement between Mercosul and the EU and worked to defeat rival projects like the U.S.-sponsored Free Trade Area of the Americas (FTAA).[64]

Due to frictions within Mercosul (discussed in greater detail below), President Lula has also pursued parallel integration projects. The Integration of Regional Infrastructure in South America (IIRSA) project features a web of transportation corridors, energy conduits, and other projects designed to facilitate flows of goods and people across the continent's rugged terrain. While President Chávez has been very active in promoting this project, Brazilian officials appear to calculate that his enthusiasm will simply defray the cost of an initiative that will inevitably redound to the benefit of the continent's largest economy. Complementing IIRSA is the Union of South American Nations (UNASUR), a relatively new body that Brazilian diplomats view as a forum for dispute resolution and, eventually, cooperation on a range of political and security issues. UNASUR is particularly attractive to Brasilia because it offers a multilateral forum for managing President Chávez's intermittent outbursts and provocations, and because it excludes Washington and thereby makes Brazil the dominant player.[65]

Brazilian officials thus envision integration as a multistep, multilevel process that will eventually encompass political and security issues as well as economic and commercial affairs. "The first stage is commercial integration," said one Defense Ministry official in 2004. "After that comes the macroeconomic one, and the military stage will be the roof of the edifice."[66] Brazilian officials portrayed the UN stabilization mission in Haiti as an embryo for South American defense cooperation, and President Lula was the driving force behind the creation of the South American Defense Council (CDS). The CDS is a still-nascent project that may eventually lead to more military-to-military contacts, more combined exercises, more collaboration on drug trafficking and other common threats, and less U.S. influence in South American defense affairs. "The geopolitical stance [the region] confronts," Minister Jobim said in March 2008, "whether we admit it or not, is the set of old continental concepts emanating from the U.S." Just as important, Brazil sees CDS as a first step toward creating a regional defense industry. Combined with Brazil's growing technological capabilities, progress on this front will allow Brasilia to become a major supplier to South American militaries, with all the influence that entails.[67]

EVALUATING BRAZILIAN GRAND STRATEGY: ACCOMPLISHMENTS AND DILEMMAS

President Lula's grand strategy has thus featured a sophisticated, multipronged approach to international affairs. It has also featured a seemingly unshakeable confidence that the geopolitical scales are tilting sharply in Brazil's favor. Brazil was not "born to spend its whole life as an emerging country," said President Lula in 2003. "I am not going to throw away this chance."[68]

Certainly, Brazil's geopolitical position is much stronger than that of just a decade ago, and President Lula's diplomatic activism has had much to do with this. His efforts to coordinate Third World positions in the WTO have made Brazil an increasingly powerful player in that body, allowing it to block trade measures deemed disadvantageous to its interests and win concessions on issues such as licensing of AIDS drugs. The G-20 has effectively replaced the G-8 as the primary forum for international economic discussions, and President Lula's outspoken participation in these debates is a chief reason why Brazil is set to translate its growing economic power into a larger voting share in the IMF and World Bank in 2011. In addition, closer attention to relations with China, France, and other "strategic partners" has helped diversify Brazilian commerce and enabled upgrades in Brazil's military, technological, and defense-industrial capabilities.

Brazil's international image has also undergone a striking transformation. A decade ago, it was highly implausible that Brazil would soon be recognized as an emerging great power. In the time since, President Lula has positioned Brazil as a leading moderate critic of U.S. hegemony, raised his country's profile through participation in forums like BRIC and IBSA, and used Brazil's status as a democratic developing country to accrue significant diplomatic capital. Through his frenetic diplomacy and cultivation of numerous strategic relationships, President Lula seems already to have achieved what many past Brazilian leaders aspired to—general recognition that their country is a key player in the international balance. "Who today could imagine solving the problems of the world without Brazil?" asked France's Nikolas Sarkozy in 2008. Similarly, in 2008 then-U.S. assistant secretary of state Thomas Shannon commented that in the 21st century, "how we work with Brazil is going to be as important as how we work with China and how we work with India." Given Brazil's longstanding quest for stature, these comments represent no mean achievement on President Lula's part.[69]

Finally, President Lula's diplomacy has created a web of relationships that his successors may be able to exploit. At the regional level, the creation of UNASUR and CSD and the expansion of Mercosul have, at the very least, provided the institutional basis for future integration under Brazilian auspices. At the global level, the IBSA and BRIC forums provide settings for the potential consolidation and expansion of South-South ties, and President Lula's various strategic partnerships offer avenues for strengthening relations with other middle powers and emerging nations. If nothing else, President Lula will leave the presidents that come after him with a wide array of possibilities and significant diplomatic flexibility.

Yet a sober evaluation of President Lula's policies must deal with their weaknesses as well as their accomplishments. While Brazilian foreign policy has seemingly gone from success to success over the past several years, over the medium and long term, the country faces four potent grand strategic dilemmas that could compromise its influence or otherwise complicate its ascent.

Economic, Social, and Political Constraints.

The first of these dilemmas has less to do with the particularities of President Lula's grand strategy than with the internal dynamics — political, social, and economic — required to sustain a forceful, effective diplomacy. Macroeconomic strength, internal cohesion, and a political system capable of producing these attributes are base-level conditions for generating national power in the global system. In certain respects, Brazil seems well positioned to meet this challenge over the long term, especially when compared to other middle powers and emerging states. Unlike China or Russia, Brazil has a genuine, multiparty democracy. Unlike India, its society is not blighted by persistent communal or religious violence. While Brazil cannot compete economically with China or the United States, the last two Brazilian presidential administrations have done quite well in maintaining economic stability, lowering poverty through targeted social spending, and enabling greater domestic consumption. The validity of the Brazilian economic model seemed to be confirmed in 2008-09, as several studies showed that the middle class had grown to encompass roughly half the population. More recently, Brazil was one of the last nations to go into recession as a result of the global financial crisis and one of the first to come out.[70]

Yet there is a compelling case to be made that Brazil has not yet achieved the strong, sustained growth necessary to match the expansive ambitions that have driven its grand strategy over the past decade. Since the debt crisis of the 1980s, Brazil has been an economic laggard in terms of overall growth rates. According to the World Bank, GDP grew at just 1.9 percent from 1987-97 and 2.8 percent from 1997-2007, considerably slower than the average rate for Latin American countries and for the broader developing world.[71] Brazilian growth rates improved in 2007 and 2008 and recent oil discoveries have fueled immense economic optimism, but the long-term trend lines are still unclear. Projections that Brazil will become the fifth-largest economy in the world by 2050 are based on the presumption that, through good policy and good fortune, the country's economy will grow substantially faster than it has over the past 2 decades. According to Roopa Puroshothaman, whose 2003 paper popularized the term "BRICs," "Brazil's performance would have to improve quite significantly relative to the past" in order to meet this expectation.[72]

Brazil's slower-than-desired growth is often attributed to high interest rates, which have remained elevated as a guard against inflation. The problem, however, runs much deeper than this. The Brazilian economy has traditionally been constrained by a maze of regulation and red tape, and even with recent reforms, there remain immense barriers to the sort of entrepreneurial activity that produces sustained growth. On nearly every major marker of entrepreneurial competitiveness—tax rates, time spent paying taxes, time spent dealing with government officials, the number of days and permits required to start a business, time required to clear direct imports and exports through customs, and many others—the Brazilian economy rates considerably worse than the Latin American average. Payroll taxes reach a stifling 60 percent, discouraging expansion and pushing many small and medium enterprises into the informal sector, where they are locked out of formal capital markets and do not contribute to the government's fiscal base.[73] The advantage of high tax rates is that they have allowed

Brazil to mobilize a comparatively large chunk of GDP for government use; the downside is that these high costs and cumbersome regulations have restricted innovation and allowed the perpetuation of a bloated, inefficient bureaucracy. Additionally, Brazil's long-term potential for growth is limited by the fact that educational reforms have not kept pace with other social programs, and so while more children are attending school, they are not necessarily acquiring the knowledge or skills that will allow them to become more productive than their parents.[74]

Infrastructural deficiencies pose an additional challenge. Brazil's ability to export efficiently, as well as to develop its large internal market, is hindered by the immense difficulty of transporting goods across the country's rough terrain. The rail system is under-developed, and as of 2004, only some 10 percent of the country's 1.74 million kilometers of roads were paved (and more than half of that 10 percent were one-lane roads). The ports are outdated and over-saturated, despite the modernization program launched under President Cardoso, meaning that stocks often sit on the docks for 3 weeks or more before being shipped. All this deters export-oriented firms from expanding and thereby creating new jobs and greater prosperity.[75]

Economists generally agree that addressing these problems will require sizable investments in education and infrastructure and, more importantly, major structural reforms designed to spur innovation, decrease regulation, and lessen the burdens of doing business. Unfortunately, the current characteristics of the political system conspire against such measures. The electoral system over-represents small parties with parochial interests, making it all the more difficult to forge the broad coalitions necessary to support sweeping structural changes. Corruption remains rampant, as illustrated by two massive payoff scandals during President Lula's first term, and powerful interests such as government bureaucracies and state-owned companies like Petrobras have a vested interest in preserving the status quo.[76] All this has weakened the impetus for structural reform, and according to one leading survey, Brazil is actually getting worse in terms of economic competitiveness. Brazil fell from 127th to 129th in "ease of doing business" from 2009 to 2010, and it suffered similar declines with respect to "ease of paying taxes" and "ease of starting a business."[77] The macroeconomic consequences of this weakness have so far been mitigated by large government stimulus packages, but Brazil's declining competitiveness and failure to implement the required reforms speak ill of its long-term economic prospects.

If Brazil cannot achieve and sustain higher levels of growth, it could eventually face several barriers to its geopolitical designs. Low growth rates would mean fewer resources for military modernization, development projects, and diplomatic initiatives abroad. They could also sap the national confidence that President Lula has tapped into, causing Brazilian politicians to argue that the country should concentrate on getting its own affairs in order. This may already be happening, in fact; José Serra, the presidential candidate put forward by the centrist Brazilian Social Democratic Party—PSDB—has argued for a more restrained foreign policy and greater attention to economic and political problems at home. Finally, because robust economic growth will be necessary to bring about additional reductions in poverty, a Brazil that lags in these categories could face resurgent class and social cleavages that might limit its internal cohesion—and thus its geopolitical potential.[78] Oil money may ease some of these potential dislocations, but given price volatility, relying primarily on an expected petroleum windfall is a gamble, not a strategy.

The economy is not the only internal issue that could retard Brazil's ascent. The country also faces a stern test of its domestic security capabilities in the form of the large, well-armed gangs that dominate huge stretches of major cities like Rio de Janeiro and Sao Paulo. These gangs generally have ties to the drug trade and a variety of illicit economic networks, and in many *favelas* they are so powerful that police, reporters, and other unwelcome visitors enter only at the risk of death. The potentially devastating impact of this insecurity came into sharp relief in May 2006, when hundreds of attacks by one such gang, the First Capital Command (PCC) of São Paulo, resulted in dozens of deaths and millions of dollars in damages, and threw South America's largest city into chaos. "The sad reality," remarked one observer "is that the state is now the prisoner of the PCC."[79]

Crime detracts from economic performance, because it forces both public and private institutions to channel resources to security-related initiatives rather than development-oriented endeavors. It also accentuates festering social divisions. The rich can afford protection—living in gated communities, hiring security guards, and bulletproofing their cars. The poor, by contrast, must live with insecurity and make accommodations with whatever criminal group dominates the neighborhood. All this reinforces deep-seated social inequities, lessens the prospects for greater social cohesion, and detracts from the legitimacy of the democratic state. If crime continues unchecked, it may become more common to hear Brazilians ask why their country should worry about projecting power abroad when it cannot even control its territory or protect its citizens at home. This question will be even harder to answer if President Lula's successors cannot resolve the other dilemmas his grand strategy entails.

Region Formation: Costs and Contradictions.

Perhaps the most important of these dilemmas involves Brazil's region-formation efforts. For all of President Lula's attempts to build a consensus behind the idea of Brazilian leadership in South America, bilateral disputes and a general sense of unease still pervade Brazil's relations with many neighbors. There are recurring tensions with Paraguay over the Itaipú hydroelectric project, with Ecuador over Brazilian investments in that country, and with Bolivia over its oil and gas industries. Venezuela has continually sought to hijack the regional diplomatic agenda, sometimes through meetings of UNASUR and CSD, bodies that President Lula played a key role in creating. Even more revealing, key regional players like Colombia and Argentina have consistently opposed President Lula's bid for a permanent seat on the Security Council, with the Argentine foreign minister calling Brazil's position on this issue "elitist and not very democratic."[80] Brazilian officials may talk about forging "strategic partnerships" with their neighbors, but President Lula's efforts to claim regional leadership still inspire more hostility than support.

Some of this resistance is simply a residue of long-standing diplomatic rivalries. Given Brazil's history of predominance in South America, it is only natural that President Lula's counterparts have been uncomfortable with his increasing assertiveness. Also, in light of President Chávez's determination to claim regional leadership for himself, a degree of conflict between Caracas and Brasilia should be expected.

Yet the travails of Brazil's South American diplomacy also reveal a fundamental contradiction within President Lula's region formation project—the fact that Brazil has so far been unwilling to pay the costs associated with achieving this objective. As several political scientists have noted, region formation is inherently an expensive and burdensome undertaking. For a middle power to be accepted as a regional leader, it must provide meaningful benefits to the smaller countries whose support it desires to enlist. These benefits can come in the form of public goods like military security, or they may be economic transfers to offset the asymmetries—the uneven accrual of gains to the larger members—that inevitably accompany economic integration projects. Additionally, to convince its neighbors that region formation is not simply domination in another guise, middle powers are generally well advised to surrender some of their own sovereignty to judicial or legislative bodies charged with resolving regional disputes. In its crudest terms, region formation is therefore a transactional relationship that imposes real costs—whether military, economic, or other—on the aspiring power.[81]

Under President Cardoso and President Lula, the Brazilian political class has refused to make this commitment. For all the talk of building relationships within South America, there remains a fear in Brazilian foreign policy circles that neighboring countries may exploit insecurity in the Amazon for their own ends. More important, because political elites are so focused on promoting and sustaining Brazil's economic development, the majority have shown little interest in schemes that would divert Brazilian resources to fostering the development of neighboring countries. Brazil still offers much less in the way of economic aid or preferential trade deals than does Venezuela. Brazilian officials have also sought to keep the price that Brazil pays for Bolivian gas and Paraguayan hydroelectric power below market rates, despite the frustration this policy has produced in those countries. Even as Brazilian diplomats have called for closer commercial ties with South America, the industrial and manufacturing communities have resisted tariff reductions (within Mercosul as well as in bilateral trading relationships) that would open the economy to greater competition and thereby impinge upon their own interests. The net result of all this has been to ensure that even as President Lula argues that economic and political integration will be good for the region as a whole, many of Brazil's neighbors remain unconvinced.[82]

This situation is most pronounced within Mercosul, where Brazil has strongly resisted demands for greater power sharing and a more equitable distribution of economic gains. Since its founding, Mercosul has been plagued by a fundamental asymmetry: Because Brazil's economy dwarfs that of the other members, these countries run huge trade deficits with Brasilia. This "original sin" has long provoked discontent within the group, but Brazilian officials have been understandably loath to assuage these concerns if it means surrendering their country's economic advantage.[83] Brazilian industrialists decry any proposal to make trade concessions to other Mercosul members. A "convergence fund" known as the *Fundo para a Convergência Estrutural e Fortalecimento Institucional do Mercosul* (FOCEM) was recently created to pay for development projects within the bloc, but it is widely acknowledged to be inadequate.[84] President Lula did take a meaningful step toward righting persistent economic asymmetries when he signed an agreement giving Paraguay a greater share of the benefits from the Itaipú dam, but it soon became clear that the Brazilian Senate had no intention of approving the pact. Nor has Brazil agreed to the establishment of strong arbitration mechanisms that would wield supranational authority over Mercosul members, something that Uruguay and Paraguay insist is crucial to ensuring a fairer distribution of trade and economic gains.[85] When it comes to regional integration, President Lula's diplomats talk in terms of the common good, but their actions bespeak a more parochial commitment to Brazilian self-interest.

As a result, Mercosul has hardly lived up to its billing as the centerpiece of President Lula's regional diplomacy. With Brazil unwilling to take the lead in redressing inequities within the pact, there has been regress rather than progress in efforts to deepen regional economic integration. Nontariff barriers are on the rise and Mercosul members have carved out exceptions to tariff reductions to protect favored economic sectors. Paraguay refuses to do away with the "double charge" (charging a tariff on goods that entered the trade zone through another member country) because its leaders reason that Brazil and Argentina will not help them compensate for the loss of customs revenue.[86] There is no effective mechanism for resolving intra-bloc disputes; Mercosul's governing institutions are so weak that Argentina and Uruguay took a recent economic disagreement to the International Court of Justice for adjudication. Not surprisingly, dissatisfaction with the pact is mounting among its smaller members. Uruguayan officials have openly discussed leaving Mercosul in favor of a free trade agreement with the United States, and Paraguayan commentators have called Mercosul "fat, useless, and interfering." Argentina has also expressed displeasure with Brazilian trade policies.[87] In concept, Mercosul may be the foundation for Brazil's consensual hegemony project, but in practice, it is an increasingly fractious and hollow organization.

The same dynamic is playing out across the region, where there is a strong sense that Brazil is trying to establish a dominant position without providing anything in return. The leaders of Chile and Argentina voiced precisely this complaint when they quit a Brazilian-led summit in 2005. According to one account, "Argentine President Nestor Kirchner stormed away from the meeting room with loud complaints about Brazil's unwillingness to shoulder the costs of leading."[88] Because Brazil is not seen to be contributing to the common good, South American officials tend to see its drive for greater international power as threatening rather than reassuring. Several countries along Brazil's Amazonian frontiers have expressed concern with President Lula's military buildup; Bolivian vice-president Álvaro Garcia Linera said that it was Brasilia, rather than Washington, that posed the greatest threat to his country.[89] Brazilian officials have exacerbated the bad feelings with a series of missteps, including accidental military incursions into Paraguay and the holding of a war game clearly meant to intimidate the Paraguayan government around the time of the Itaipú negotiations in mid-2009.[90]

Because Brazil has failed to bring its mooted South American constituency into line, it has struggled to defeat rival leadership projects in the region. While President Chávez is not well liked in many South American countries, discomfort with President Lula's foreign policies has helped create a vacuum that the Venezuelan leader has been able to fill with his petroleum diplomacy. Bolivia and Ecuador have become members of ALBA, and President Chávez's purchase of billions of dollars of Argentine debt has given him some influence with that country. On the other side of the political spectrum, a group of nations led by Peru, Colombia, Chile, and Mexico is pursuing a project known as the Pacific Arc, which can be seen as an effort to balance against both Venezuela and Brazil.[91] Many of these same countries—most notably Colombia and Peru—have also moved closer to the United States, and Uruguayan president Tabaré Vázquez sent a shock through Mercosul in 2006-07 when he indicated that he wished to sign an FTA with Washington (he ultimately settled for a trade and investment framework accord).[92]

In short, Brazilian officials can hardly claim that South America is united, much less that it is united behind Brazilian leadership. If President Lula's successors do not make Brazil's bid for regional hegemony more attractive to its neighbors, they too will find it difficult to establish a strong power base in Brazil's backyard.

Global Coalitions and Strategic Partnerships: Tensions and Limitations.

The third dilemma has to do with the strategic partnerships and global coalitions that President Lula has sought to establish. As discussed previously, the rationale for this activity has been that these groups will broaden Brazil's strategic options, provide leverage in dealing with the United States and the West, and allow Brazilian officials to position themselves as spokesmen for the developing world. This strategy has racked up some initial successes over the past several years. Looking ahead, however, there are serious questions as to whether these partnerships will be cohesive or effective enough to serve as meaningful force-multipliers for Brazilian diplomatic influence.

Consider, for instance, President Lula's efforts to build international support for his Security Council campaign through a variety of bilateral and multilateral endeavors. Groups like the G-4 and IBSA have made Security Council reform a defining theme of their diplomacy, and individual countries like France and the United Kingdom have pledged their backing for Brazil's candidacy. Yet Brazil still faces considerable challenges in achieving permanent membership, and not only because Security Council reform is inherently fraught with difficulty. Brazil's bid lacks credibility due to the fact that major Latin American countries—Mexico, Argentina, and Colombia—oppose it, and President Lula has encountered foot-dragging and obstinacy from several of his strategic partners as well. The Russian government is loath to dilute its global influence by expanding one of the relatively few elite international clubs to which it still belongs.[93] China is unalterably opposed to the program of the G-4, owing to Beijing's long-standing antipathy toward Japan and its continuing rivalry with India. So far, Brazilian diplomats have failed to budge Beijing from this stance. When President Lula designated China a full market economy in 2004 in order to ease restrictions on Chinese imports, the expected payoff, Chinese support for Brazil's Security Council bid, was not forthcoming. Solidarity among the rising powers is one thing; cold national interest is another.[94]

This split between Russia, Brazil, and China casts doubt on the notion that the peripheral powers are natural allies in their struggle against U.S. hegemony. It also touches on the limited cohesiveness of the BRIC forum. Although BRIC serves as an attractive academic paradigm for grouping several rising states, the frenzy of BRIC diplomacy and summitry over the past several years has in many ways obscured the fact that the group is beset by numerous fissures. Its members have widely divergent conceptions of governance and legitimacy, raising questions as to the compatibility of their long-term visions of the international order. The four economies are also less complementary than is often supposed.[95] Brazilian manufacturers have already identified Chinese imports as an unwelcome source of low-priced competition, leading President Lula's government to impose new restrictions on Chinese goods. Furthermore, Brazilian economic officials are finding that they face the same problem that has long bedeviled their American counterparts: that China's efforts to keep its currency low hurt Brazilian exports and make it more difficult to Brazilian industries to compete with Chinese imports.[96] As these frictions indicate, while bilateral trade between the various BRIC countries has risen substantially, the trade policies of these nations remain quite disparate. This being the case, predictions that the group is on its way to becoming a functioning trade bloc or an alternative center of economic gravity are premature.

Even if Brazil can maintain strong bilateral ties with Russia, China, and India—and as the above indicates, this outcome is hardly assured—the BRIC group as a whole will likely become more fractious over time.

India, Russia, and China are natural rivals rather than natural partners, given their geographic proximity to one another, and competition within this subgroup is already on the rise. Many Russian strategists see the growing strategic, economic, and demographic challenge from China as more threatening than anything in Moscow's relations with the United States.[97] Indian officials are hardly sanguine about China's search for a port on the Indian Ocean (especially given that this search is leading Beijing toward India's rival, Pakistan, and its authoritarian neighbor, Myanmar) and the need to obtain oil supplies from Africa could soon emerge as another point of friction.[98] As the individual BRIC countries — especially China and India — become more powerful, they will probably become more assertive in pressing their particular national interests, which may bode ill for intra-group harmony. Peering out over the next decade and beyond, BRIC looks like a shaky foundation upon which to base any coalition-building strategy.

In some ways, IBSA seems to be a more realistic option. Its members are all multicultural democracies, and the geographical distance between them dampens potential intragroup rivalries. Here too, rhetoric has outpaced reality in terms of both internal cohesion and concrete diplomatic or economic accomplishment. It is highly questionable whether IBSA can gain acceptance as the voice of the developing nations; calls to "democratize" international institutions ring hollow with many of the Third World countries that the group claims to represent. The prospect that the IBSA three might achieve permanent standing on the Security Council seems decidedly undemocratic and even threatening to countries like Nigeria, Pakistan, Argentina, and Colombia.[99]

On the economic front, trade between members has soared over the past decade, and there is room for greater cooperation on issues like energy and investment. There are also, however, high barriers to meaningful economic or trade integration. The dearth of transportation links between the three countries makes shipping expensive and lessens comparative advantage.[100] While this issue can potentially be resolved over time, it may be more difficult to overcome the policy differences that separate the IBSA countries. India's economy is protected by much higher tariff barriers than either Brazil's or South Africa's, and despite Minister Amorim's claim that IBSA can "speak with one voice" on economic matters, India and Brazil have conflicting interests on issues like agricultural policy. This has already led to splits within the group, with these two countries coming down on opposite sides of the issue at the failed Doha Round trade talks in 2008.[101]

To its credit, IBSA has been able to minimize disputes over issues like nuclear energy and nonproliferation. These compromises give some hope that the group will be able to maintain its internal cohesion and focus on the overriding objective of diversifying the global power balance. As with BRIC however, there is a degree of long-term strategic divergence at work within IBSA. The current Indian government clearly calculates that a closer partnership with the United States is important to achieving India's regional and global aims, as shown by the recent U.S.-India nuclear agreement and the subsequent tightening of relations with Washington. Moreover, as the breakdown in IBSA solidarity at the Doha Round talks in 2008 demonstrated, to the extent that these rising powers feel strong enough to stake out independent positions in international negotiations, they will probably feel less compelled to sacrifice their own interests in the name of Third-World cohesion. This does not mean that IBSA is doomed to irrelevance, but it does mean that solidifying this partnership will demand significant commitment and concessions from the three members.

As for President Lula's burgeoning relationship with Iran, the putative benefits of this initiative—a greater voice in Middle Eastern diplomacy, an opportunity to serve as a mediator between Tehran and the West, a chance to strengthen Third-World solidarity and assert Brazil's diplomatic autonomy vis-à-vis the United States—are more compelling in theory than in practice. It is hard to image that President Lula's warm treatment of President Ahmadinejad will lead to greater Brazilian influence with the Sunni Muslim and Arab states that occupy the vast majority if the Middle East. Nor is this partnership good for Brazil's image. The more President Lula defends the human rights practices and electoral legitimacy of the Iranian regime, the more he risks compromising the democratic credentials that have served him so well.[102] Then there are the implications for what is still Brazil's most important diplomatic relationship—its conflicted partnership with the United States.

Brazil-U.S. Relations: Partnership or Rivalry?

Since the mid-20th century, U.S.-Brazilian relations have typically featured a mix of conflict and collaboration. During World War II, Getulio Vargas sent Brazilian troops to fight alongside the Allies in Italy, albeit after securing promises of U.S. economic aid as the price for doing so. In the 1960s and 1970s, the pronounced anti-communism of Brazil's military governments (particularly that of Emilio Garrastazu Médici) conduced to a common interest in keeping the radical Left out of power in Latin America. "I wish he were running the whole continent," Richard Nixon said of Médici in 1971.[103] At the same time, Brazilian leaders were wary of being seen as Washington's lackey, compelling them to put distance between themselves and their U.S. counterparts. They chafed at American efforts to interfere in Brazilian politics, especially criticism of the military governments, as well as Washington's attempts to slow the postwar diffusion of global power. Brazilian governments refused to sign the nuclear Non-Proliferation Treaty through the 1980s, resisted American pressure on human rights issues under the Carter administration, and found numerous other ways to assert their diplomatic autonomy.[104]

A similar ambivalence characterizes current U.S.-Brazil relations. At the strategic level, the two countries have broadly congruent interests. Both Washington and Brasilia desire stability in Latin America and in the larger international arena. Both countries believe in the benefits of a liberal economic order, even if they differ on what exactly that order should look like. Both nations have democratic political systems, and both would be threatened should authoritarian states in Europe or Asia come to dominate the international order. With respect to the contemporary setting in Latin America, both Brazil and the United States have a vested interest in containing authoritarian populism and seeing that Chávez does not emerge as the preeminent regional statesman.

These shared interests have led to bilateral cooperation—or at least accommodation—on several important issues. Collaboration on counterterrorism and organized crime issues has generally been good. In

2007, Presidents Lula and George W. Bush signed an agreement to promote the development of a regional biofuels capacity as a counterweight to President Chávez's petro-influence. Deputy Assistant Secretary of State Christopher McMullen pointed to President Lula's administration as an exemplar of responsible, left-of-center governance in Latin America, calling it "a model for countries in the region" and a "natural regional leader and global partner."[105] For his part, President Lula has sharply criticized numerous aspects of U.S. policy in Latin America, but he has simultaneously worked to defeat the more radical positions taken by President Chávez and his allies. President Lula pushed hard for an end to the U.S. embargo against Cuba in the run-up to a regional summit in June 2009, for instance, but he ultimately helped broker a compromise that bridged the U.S. position and that of countries like Venezuela and Honduras.[106] At the level of public diplomacy, President Lula has enjoyed warm personal relationships with both former President George Bush and President Barrack Obama, and U.S. officials have been at pains to emphasize the common interests that unite the two countries.[107] Military cooperation has grown, with both countries providing students, visitors and lecturers to each other's conferences and educational institutions.

Yet there is also a growing degree of conflict inherent in President Lula's foreign policy and the growth of Brazilian power. At the most parochial level, the need to placate the more left-wing elements of President Lula's Workers Party (PT) coalition has occasionally compelled the president to make anti-imperialist, anti-U.S. themes prominent in his public discourse.[108] More substantively, many Brazilian observers believe that the current rules of international trade and finance are prejudicial to their country's development, and that these rules are thus in need of revision. And in the broadest geopolitical sense, Brazil simply cannot achieve the increased influence it seeks—whether in South America or the larger global system—without weakening that of the dominant power in these environments. Ten years ago, Brazilian officials tended to make this point obliquely; under President Lula, they have made it more explicitly. In 2008, Ambassador Antonio Patriota told a U.S. audience that "the days of the Monroe Doctrine are over," and other commentators have taken an even more confrontational tone. "Brazil is at war," opined the *Folha de Sao Paulo,* a nationalist newspaper. "A diplomatic war, with a clear strategy and coherent tactics, against the unipolar world. Nothing personal against the United States, but entirely against a single power hovering above all, in every area."[109]

Quietly but unmistakably, this strategic tension has moved to the center of U.S.-Brazil relations. As discussed above, Brazilian diplomats have emerged as foils for their U.S. counterparts in international trade forums, often serving as focal points for resistance to Washington's proposals. President Lula seized the Iraq war as an opportunity to rally diplomatic opposition to U.S. hegemony, a project he has since continued through IBSA, BRIC, and other forums. At the bilateral level, President Lula continually proclaims the injustice of the U.S. tariff on ethanol imports, and this issue intrudes on virtually every encounter between high-level officials. As Brazil has become more confident, it has also become more defiant, and this is ineluctably causing friction with the United States.[110]

This same tendency is also apparent within South America, where the shared imperative of containing

President Chávez has masked the increasingly competitive tenor of U.S.-Brazilian relations. President Lula's opposition to the FTAA derived largely from the fear that the project would link South American countries to the U.S. economy and thereby break up the "solid, regional space" that his administration aimed to construct.[111] Similarly, the creation of institutions like UNASUR and CSD must be seen as efforts to balance U.S. influence in South America by making Brazil, rather than Washington, the region's dominant interlocutor on political and defense matters. Along these lines, Brasilia has worked to limit the U.S. defense presence in the region. President Lula sharply criticized the U.S.-Colombia basing deal signed in 2009, and at a UNASUR meeting shortly thereafter, he led several countries in trying to limit the type of activities that could be carried out at the bases. "Dear friend Obama," he remarked, "we don't need U.S. bases in Colombia to fight drug trafficking in South America. We can take care of fighting drug trafficking within our borders and you must take care of your drug users."[112] The "reactivation" of the U.S. 4th Fleet in 2008 also caused a strong response, with President Lula speculating that American naval forces constituted a threat to Brazil's offshore oil reserves.[113] Brazil seeks to displace the United States as the dominant power in South America, and this objective brings with it an elevated risk of bilateral conflict.

This budding rivalry has recently spilled over into Central America, even though Brazil has little hope of competing with U.S. economic and political sway on the isthmus. In 2009, President Lula took exception to what he perceived as Washington's insufficient interest in reversing the coup against Manuel Zelaya in Honduras. Marco Aurélio Garcia criticized President

Obama for declining to "put more pressure on the putschists," and President Lula eventually assumed a key role in the crisis by permitting—perhaps reluctantly—Zelaya to take refuge in the Brazilian embassy in Tegucigalpa. U.S. officials believed that this decision simply complicated prospects for a negotiated settlement to the crisis, and the State Department issued a pointed—if elliptical—critique of Brazilian policy. Brazil subsequently refused to recognize the democratically elected government that took power following elections in late 2009, although the realization that this would do nothing to change the situation on the ground has since convinced President Lula to soften his stance.[114]

The divergence of U.S. and Brazilian policies is most evident with respect to Iran, which is rapidly becoming one of the more contentious issues in the relationship. U.S. officials do not view President Lula's engagement strategy kindly and worry that Brazil is granting Tehran international legitimacy at a most inopportune time. Congressman Eliot Engel (D-NY), head of the Western Hemisphere subcommittee in the House of Representatives, gave voice to this worry, calling President Lula's decision to play host to President Ahmadinejad in late 2009 "a gross error, a terrible mistake." "It makes you wonder if Brazil is really ready for the new era of global relations it envisions," he said.[115] None of this has fazed President Lula. What is remarkable about the Brazilian president's policy is not simply that he sees strategic value in relations with Iran, but that he apparently sees diplomatic or political value in snubbing Washington on this issue. President Lula has rebutted U.S. criticisms of Iran's nuclear programs and post-election repression, and in March 2010, he denounced American efforts to impose

UN sanctions on Tehran on the eve of a visit by Secretary of State Hillary Clinton.[116] The nuclear agreement brokered by Brazil and Turkey in May 2010 was widely seen as an effort to frustrate U.S. efforts to rally international support for harsher sanctions against Iran, leading to further expressions of concern from American officials.

These points of discord indicate the essential dilemma of U.S.-Brazilian ties—the fact that shared interests do not necessarily lead to cooperative or harmonious relations. For all the commonalities that bind Brasilia and Washington, the simple fact of growing Brazilian power, combined with the moderately revisionist grand strategy that President Lula has pursued, inevitably foster elements in which the two countries' aims grate against one another. This does not mean that Brazil and the United States are headed for military conflict, which is almost unthinkable, or even outright diplomatic hostility. Yet it could eventually create a situation in which the United States sees Brazil more as a competitor than as a partner, while Brazil fears that the United States is trying to stunt its natural geopolitical growth. Such a development is less likely as long as President Chávez's activities remind U.S. and Brazilian policymakers of how much they have in common, but should this variable be removed from the equation, a downward turn in the relationship would not be particularly improbable.

The drawbacks of such a scenario—for the United States and Brazil alike—are not difficult to imagine. Brazilian diplomats will find it extremely difficult to accomplish their major diplomatic goals—a more favorable world trade system, for instance, or Security Council reform—without the cooperation or at least the acquiescence of the United States. Similarly, if

Washington sees Brazil as a rival, it could very well respond by lending additional support to Chile, Peru, Colombia, or other countries that remain aloof from President Lula's bid for regional hegemony. For the United States, on the other hand, a productive relationship with Brazil will be central to ensuring a smooth passage from unipolarity to multipolarity and maintaining a balance of power that favors democratic norms and institutions. Within the Western Hemisphere, a strained relationship with a rising Brazil could badly complicate U.S.-Latin American affairs and could eventually raise the specter of a geopolitical challenge in Washington's backyard. Beyond all this, the prospects for progress on a range of multilateral issues—from WTO talks to negotiations on climate change—hinge in substantial measure on productive dealings between the United States and Brazil. Over the next several decades, managing this relationship will therefore be a key diplomatic challenge for officials in both countries.

POLICY IMPLICATIONS FOR BRAZIL AND THE UNITED STATES

What does the foregoing analysis mean for the officials charged with crafting Brazilian strategy after President Lula, and for the U.S. diplomats with whom they will interact? Four general propositions seem most relevant. First, the trajectory of Brazil's ascent and the effectiveness of its grand strategy will depend on domestic policy as much as foreign policy. Over the past 25 years, and especially over the past 15, Brazil has made significant progress in strengthening the domestic foundations of national power by restoring macroeconomic stability, reducing poverty, establishing a vibrant democracy, and grappling seriously with pervasive social problems. Indeed, it is this progress that has given the country the confidence to act so boldly in world affairs and provided President Lula with the credibility he enjoys in global forums. Yet this domestic consolidation is still lacking in many ways, and there are a variety of outstanding economic, political, and social issues that could delay or even potentially derail Brazil's rise.

Managing this danger will require sustained, creative engagement on several fronts: economic policies that remove obstacles to investment and permit higher levels of growth; social policies that improve the quality of primary and secondary education and provide greater access to essential services; holistic anti-crime measures that reduce citizen insecurity; infrastructure projects that facilitate commerce; and political reforms that mitigate corruption and encourage greater government responsiveness on the aforementioned issues. There already exist several promising initiatives designed to address certain of these issues: an Accelerated Growth Program that reduces tax and bureaucratic burdens for qualifying businesses, "participatory budgets" that reduce opportunities for corruption in local service provision, community policing strategies that mimic counterinsurgency in focusing on cultivating and protecting the population.[117] Yet each of the internal questions listed above constitutes an immense policy challenge, and it is possible that meeting some of these challenges may require making trade-offs with respect to others. Wrestling with these issues will certainly be a long-term process, one that requires innovation and experimentation as well as an ability to resist the allure of measures that may be politically expedient but will exacerbate the structural problems the country still faces. Whether the political class rises to the occasion in dealing with these issues will go far in determining the range of possibilities open to Brazilian diplomats during the next decade and beyond.

Second, future governments will need to resolve the contradiction between Brazil's grand aims for regional leadership and its relative stinginess in promoting this project. As long as South American countries believe that Brazil is working to further its own hegemonic ambitions rather than the common good, they are unlikely to provide Brasilia with the diplomatic support or broadened regional power base it desires. Brazilian domestic opinion has generally been hostile to increasing aid or the sharing of power with the neighbors. At some point, however, policymakers and opinion-shaping elites will have to come to grips with the fact that a less parsimonious policy will be crucial to improving Brazil's image and dealing effectively with competing regional leadership claims. Initiatives like the decision to allow $21 million worth of Bolivian goods to enter the Brazilian market tariff-free in 2009 represent useful gestures, but going forward, more substantive steps will be required.[118]

Perhaps the best arena for these measures would be Mercosul, which is both the core of the consensual hegemony project and the forum in which regional power asymmetries are most pronounced. In concept, FOCEM is designed to pay for infrastructure projects that will facilitate trade and increase the export competitiveness of its members; what is needed is for Brazil (and, to some extent, Argentina) to increase these convergence payments and focus them more, if not entirely, on the poorest members of the group—particularly Paraguay.[119] Brazil should also dedicate itself to strengthening Mercosul's governing organs, not simply by vesting greater powers in the parliament, but also by developing an effective supranational judicial institution from which the less powerful members can seek recourse in the inevitable event of intrabloc disputes. In the short term, taking these steps will mean surrendering some of Brazil's sovereignty and national advantage. Over the long term, these measures will be essential to easing tensions within the group and building an attractive model of regional integration under Brazilian leadership.

Working toward this outcome will require a greater resource commitment, which leads to a third imperative of Brazilian strategy — the need for more systematic resource production and prioritization. As mentioned above, Brazil needs to mobilize more resources — both political and economic — to address its deep-seated internal problems. Additionally, although President Lula's frenzied diplomacy has served its purpose of broadening Brazil's geopolitical horizons and providing a measure of strategic flexibility, this scattershot approach to international diplomacy also runs the risk of dissipating Brazil's limited economic and diplomatic resources. This problem is especially pressing given the need for more intensive engagement within Mercosul, the limitations of global partnerships like the BRIC forum, and the fact that some of President Lula's diplomatic initiatives — his dealings with Iran, for instance — may ultimately bring more blowback than benefit.

This does not mean that President Lula's successors should abandon forums like BRIC and IBSA rather than seeking to improve them, or that it should focus exclusively on cultivating a strong regional following. Doing so would simply squander the strategic flexibility that these leaders will inherit. It means, rather, that President Lula's successors should subject his myriad diplomatic projects to harsh scrutiny, so as to identify those that are most promising and essential. This could entail deemphasizing the bid to gain a permanent seat on the Security Council, which will only become feasible once Brazil gains greater acceptance as a regional leader, and may in any case be stymied by Russian or Chinese opposition. It could also entail de-prioritizing one tenuous multilateral partnership — BRIC, for instance — so that Brazilian diplomats can devote greater energy to making IBSA a more cohesive group. Regardless of the precise formula, what is essential is that President Lula's successors choose carefully among the range of Brazil's diplomatic options so as to avoid the dispersion of resources that will eventually result from his all-encompassing approach to foreign policy.

Fourth, both U.S. and Brazilian officials need to develop coherent approaches to manage bilateral tensions and preserve a constructive partnership. In part, this goal can be achieved by identifying and focusing the bilateral relationship on areas where the two countries have convergent interests. The biofuels deal signed in 2007 exemplifies this ethos; it furthers both countries' objective of reducing Latin American energy insecurity and thereby limiting President Chávez's regional influence. A civil nuclear energy agreement modeled on the U.S.-India accord could be similarly profitable, as could an expansion of security and military ties.[120] For all the recent emphasis on constructing a "defense shield" against U.S. meddling, Brazilian security officials recognize the importance of joint projects to secure chaotic regions like the Tri-Border Area between Argentina, Paraguay, and Brazil, and there is still considerable interest in military exchanges and exercises as well as reviving a training relationship that has eroded badly since the 1970s. (Indeed, what was widely ignored amid the diplomatic squall over the reactivation of the 4th Fleet was that this measure will give the United States a better ability to interact with the Brazilian Navy on issues ranging from training and joint maneuvers to patrolling the South Atlantic.[121]) Pursuing these and other such initiatives can broaden the range of measures on which the United States and Brazil collaborate, thereby encouraging a more cooperative bilateral norm.

In the same spirit, it would behoove Washington and Brasilia to exploit issues of asymmetrical interest; in other words, issues on which a concession costs one power relatively little but benefits the other a great deal. Two of these issues are particularly salient: ethanol and Iran. Maintaining the 54-cent per gallon ethanol tariff does the United States little good economically (this tariff survives solely for domestic political reasons), and abolishing or even lowering it would provide a significant economic and diplomatic boon for Brazil. Similarly, for Brazil to distance itself somewhat from President Ahmadinejad would entail only a minimal economic or diplomatic hardship (it might actually be beneficial for Brazilian diplomacy), and it would go far in convincing U.S. officials that Brasilia aspires to be a responsible stakeholder rather than a disruptive presence. Diplomatic give-and-take is necessarily a part of any relationship between major countries; focusing on these asymmetrical issues makes giving somewhat less painful.

Finally, while dialogue is not an end in itself, it would be useful to strengthen mechanisms for policy discussion and high-level bilateral communication.

Poor communication was a factor in at least two recent bilateral disputes, those involving the Colombian bases deal in 2009 and the flap over the U.S. 4th Fleet a year earlier. Additionally, there is a broad range of issues that will require increased high-level consultation in coming years: climate change, trade disputes, the requirements of maintaining stability in Latin America, the changing global strategic panorama, and others. In 1976, Henry Kissinger and his Brazilian counterparts signed an agreement establishing just such a forum. The agreement lapsed amid the deterioration of U.S.-Brazilian relations under former President Jimmy Carter, but the current juncture offers a promising opportunity to revive the idea.[122] Doing so will not prevent the frictions that are bound to occur between the United States and a rising Brazil, but in conjunction with the other steps outlined here, it may help mitigate these conflicts and maintain a productive climate in the relationship.

CONCLUSION

Grand strategy is the relation of means to ends, the process by which nations harness and allocate resources in the service of their international objectives. Over the past 8 years, President Lula's grand strategy has exploited Brazil's moral credibility, diplomatic capabilities, and growing economic power to raise his country's profile and diversify its strategic portfolio. Yet, as President Lula's presidency comes to a close, there is still much to be done to make Brazil's foreign policy equal to its lofty aspirations. Brazil must find the resources and political will to make its regional leadership bid more credible; it must become more discerning in its global partnerships and initiatives; it must work toward a sustainable *modus vivendi* with the United States; and, above all, it must marshal the resources, creativity, and commitment to attack tenacious internal problems.

These are the tasks that fall to President Lula's successors. Brazil is undoubtedly going to play a significant part in world politics over the next century; how significant—and how constructive—will hinge on how these policymakers address the key dilemmas of Brazilian grand strategy.

ENDNOTES

1. Charles Krauthammer, "The Unipolar Moment Revisited," *National Interest,* No. 70, Winter 2002, p. 17; Fareed Zakaria, *The Post-American World,* New York: Norton, 2008; Parag Khanna, *The Second World: Empires and Influence in the New Global Order,* New York: Random House, 2008; Andrew Bacevich, *The Limits of Power: The End of American Exceptionalism,* New York: Macmillan, 2008; Paul Craig Roberts, "The End of American Hegemony," *Electric Politics,* October 2008, available from *www.electricpolitics. com/2008/10/the_end_of_american_hegemony.html.*

2. "Brazil Must Think Big, Says Jobim," *Latin American Regional Report: Brazil & Southern Cone,* July 2009; "Lula Launches Preparations for Superpower Status," *Latin American Security & Strategic Review,* September 2007.

3. As stated previously, some of the initiatives that have figured in President Lula's grand strategy originated under his predecessors. Because President Lula has dominated Brazilian politics and foreign policy since 2003, however, and because he has pursued such an ambitious project to increase Brazilian power and influence, it makes sense to speak of "Lula's grand strategy."

4. For laudatory appraisals, see David Rothkopf, "The World's Best Foreign Minister," *Foreign Policy Online,* October 7, 2009, available from *www.foreignpolicy.com;* Leticia Pinheiro, "Celso Amorim: Right Man, Right Place, Right Time," *World Poli-*

tics Review, February 2, 2010, available from *www.wpr.com*; Kellie Meiman and David Rothkopf, *The United States and Brazil: Two Perspectives on Dealing with Partnership and Rivalry*, Washington, DC: Center for American Progress, March 2009.

5. The quotes are from Ronald Schneider, *Brazil: Culture and Politics in a New Industrial Powerhouse,* Boulder, CO: Westview Press, 1996, p. 215; Paulo Sotero and Leslie Elliott Armijo, "Brazil: To Be or Not to Be a BRIC?" *Asian Perspective,* Vol. 31, No. 4, Spring 2007, p. 54.

6. Lecture Delivered by Antônio F. Azeredo da Silveira, March 4, 1975, 20-BRA-1-3, Foreign Ministry Files, Library and Archives Canada.

7. Kissinger, quoted in Hal Brands, "Third World Politics in an Age of Global Turmoil: The Latin American Challenge to U.S. and Western Hegemony, 1965-1975," *Diplomatic History,* Vol. 32, No. 1, January 2008, p. 130; George F. Kennan, *Around the Cragged Hill: A Personal and Political Philosophy,* New York: Norton, 1993, p. 143.

8. Jim O'Neill, the Goldman Sachs analyst who helped popularize the term "BRIC," recalls that at one meeting with Latin American investors, the man who introduced him said, "We all know that the only reason the B is there is because without it, there is no acronym." See Gillian Tett, "The Story of the BRICs," *Financial Times,* January 15, 2010.

9. See Fernando Henrique Cardoso, *A Arte da Política: A História que Vivi (The Art of Politics: The Story that I Lived)*, Rio de Janeiro, Brazil: Civilização Brasileira, 2006, pp. 604-606, 616-618. The Spanish-language acronym for the South American trade bloc is *Mercosur,* which is often the version used in the sources cited below.

10. As of December 2009, Brazil was involved in peacekeeping or stabilization missions in Haiti, Chad, the Central African Republic, Western Sahara, Cyprus, Liberia, Nepal, Sudan, East Timor, and Cote D'Ivoire. Information on these and previous commitments is available from *www.un.org/en/peacekeeping/contributors/06-08.shtml.*

11. Quoted in Jens Glusing, "Brazil Flexes Muscles over Honduras Crisis," *Der Spiegel Online,* October 9, 2009. On the state of Brazilian democracy and social programs, see Martin Ravallion, "A Comparative Perspective on Poverty Reduction in Brazil, China, and India," Washington, DC: World Bank Development Research Group, October 2009; Lourdes Sola, "Politics, Markets, and Society in Lula's Brazil," *Journal of Democracy,* Vol. 19, No. 2, April 2008, pp. 31-45.

12. The World Bank ranks Brazil ninth in terms of GDP at purchasing power parity as of 2007. Other organizations have listed Brazil as high as eighth or as low as tenth. See World Bank, "Brazil Country Brief," January 26, 2010, available from *web. worldbank.org/WBSITE/EXTERNAL/COUNTRIES/LACEXT/BRAZ ILEXTN/0,,menuPK:322351~pagePK:141132~piPK:141107~theSite PK:322341,00.html.*

13. See Roopa Puroshothaman, "Dreaming with BRICs: The Path to 2050," Goldman Sachs Economic Paper No. 99, October 2003, p. 4; also "Brazil Can Reach Developed Country Status by 2016," *Latin American Regional Report: Brazil & Southern Cone,* January 2010. Brazil's economic prospects and their geopolitical implications are discussed further below.

14. "Oil: Brazil's 'Second Independence,'" *Latin American Regional Report: Brazil & Southern Cone,* May 2009; "Brazil: Petrobras Euphoria Fades With Oil Price," *Oxford Analytica,* December 11, 2008.

15. "Mr. Luiz Inácio Lula da Silva, President of the Federal Republic of Brazil," Address to the Council on Foreign Relations, September 25, 2003; available from *www.cfr.org/publication/6563/ mr_luiz_incio_lula_da_silva_president_of_the_federal_republic_of_ brazil.html.*

16. On the global benefits of American hegemony, see Michael Mandelbaum, *The Case for Goliath: How America Works as the World's Government in the Twenty-First Century,* New York: Public Affairs, 2006.

17. "Brazilian President Seeks More Clout for Countries like His," *CNN.com,* March 25, 2009; also see Secretaria de Assuntos Estratégicos, "Amorim destaca protagonismo internacional do Brasil" ("Amorim Emphasizes Brazil's International Protagonism"), February 25, 2010, available from *www.sae.gov.br/site/?p=2898.*

18. "Taking Advantage of the 4th Fleet Syndrome," *Latin American Security & Strategic Review,* August 2008; see also "Lecture by the Foreign Minister of Brazil, Ambassador Celso Amorim, Given at the London School of Economics on 17 March 2004," available from *www.brazil.org/uk/press/speeches.*

19. "Speech by the President of Brazil, Luiz Inácio Lula da Silva, at the Plenary Meeting of the 61st UN General Assembly in New York, September 19, 2006," available from *www.brazil.org.uk/press/speeches.*

20. Brazil's role in obstructing the Doha Round is discussed in greater detail in the section on the components of Brazilian foreign policy.

21. Gary Duffy, "Brazil's Lula Raps 'White' Crisis," *BBC News,* March 27, 2009; Jamil Chade, "Amorim diz que ricos mentem como Goebbels" ("Amorim says that the rich lie like Goebbels"), *O Estado de São Paulo,* July 20, 2008.

22. "MINUSTAH and Its Significance," *Latin American Security & Strategic Review,* July 2003.

23. "Brazil's Foreign Policy under Lula," *Latin American Special Report,* May 2004.

24. "Lecture by the Foreign Minister of Brazil, Ambassador Celso Amorim, Given at the London School of Economics on March 17, 2004."

25. "'Assertive' Bid to Change Power Balance," *Latin American Security & Strategic Review,* October 2003.

26. "Discurso do Presidente da República, Luiz Inácio Lula da Silva, em almoço oferecido aos formandos do Instituto Rio Branco" ("Speech by the President of the Republic, Luiz Inácio Lula da

Silva, at the lunch offered to the graduating students of the Rio Branco Institute"), September 18, 2003, available from *www.mre. gov.br/portugues/politica_externa/discursos.*

27. See John Mearsheimer, *The Tragedy of Great Power Politics,* New York: Norton, 2001, chaps. 3-4.

28. "Brazil Must Think Big, Says Jobim."

29. "France's Sarkozy in Brazil," *Latin American Regional Report: Brazil and Southern Cone,* January 2009; "Brazil's Pursuit of a Nuclear Submarine Raises Proliferation Concerns," *WMD Insights,* March 2008, available from *www.wmdinsights.com/I23/I23_LA1_BrazilPursuit.htm.*

30. E. Peter Wittkopf, "Brazil's SIVAM: Surveillance against Crime and Terrorism," *International Journal of Intelligence and Counterintelligence,* Vol. 16, No. 4, October 2003, pp. 543-560; "Amazonia, uma fronteira desguarnecida"("Amazonia, An Ungarrisoned Border"), *O Globo,* April 20, 2008.

31. Jobim, quoted in "Arms Transfers as Instruments of Foreign Policy," *Latin American Security & Strategic Review,* October 2009; "Paper: Argentina and Brazil Eye Nuclear Sub," *Business Week,* February 25, 2008; "Aliança com a Russia" ("Alliance with Russia"), *Defesa BR,* available from *www.defesabr.com/MD/md_russia.htm.*

32. "Brazil," *Jane's World Armies,* Issue 20, 2008, p. 92; Luiz Inácio Lula da Silva, *Política de Defesa Nacional* (National Defense Policy), June 30, 2005, available from *www.defesa.gov.br/mobilizacao/arquivos/decreto_politica_defesa_nacional.pdf;*"Brasil prepara simulacro de guerra dirigido al Paraguay" ("Brazil Prepares Wargame Directed at Paraguay"), *ABC Digital,* November 13, 2009. The threat posed by urban crime is discussed in Alvaro de Souza Pinheiro, *Irregular Warfare: Brazil's Fight against Criminal Urban Guerrillas,* Hurlburt Field, FL: Joint Special Operations University, September 2009.

33. Quoted in "Taking Advantage of the 4th Fleet Syndrome," *Latin American Security & Strategic Review,* August 2008; also da Silva, *Política de Defesa Nacional;* "Interstate Conflict in Latin

America: A Thing of the Past," *Latin American Special Report,* April 2007.

34. Xando Pereira, ""Precisamos de um Sivam Que Funcione no Mar" ("We Need a SIVAM that Functions in the Sea"), *A Tarde,* September 4, 2008, available from *www.atarde.com.br/jornalatarde/ politica/noticia.jsf?id=953244.*

35. The quotes are from "Taking Advantage of the 4th Fleet Syndrome"; Xando Pereira, "Precisamos de um Sivam Que Funcione no Mar" ("We Need a SIVAM that Functions in the Sea"), *A Tarde,* September 4, 2008, available from *www.atarde.com.br/ jornalatarde/politica/noticia.jsf?id=953244;* "Reviving the Idea of a Subregional Defense Council," *Latin American Security & Strategic Review,* March 2008.

36. On South American defense spending, see "Chile Per Capita Expenditure on Defense, the Highest of Latin America," *MercoPress,* March 16, 2010.

37. On this point, consult Puroshothaman, "Dreaming with BRICs."

38. Robert Keohane, "Liliputians' Dilemmas: Small States in International Politics," *International Organization,* Vol. 23, No. 2, Spring 1969, pp. 296-298.

39. For a discussion of soft balancing, see Robert Pape, "Soft Balancing against the United States," *International Security,* Vol. 30, No. 1, Summer 2005, pp. 7-45.

40. S. P. Guimarães, "Los tres años del gobierno del Presidente de Brasil, Luiz Inácio Lula da Silva" ("Three Years of the Government of the President of Brazil, Luiz Inácio Lula da Silva"), *La Onda Digital,* available from *www.laondadigital.com/laonda/ laonda/201-300/277/recuadro2.htm.*

41. On this latter point, see Pape, "Soft Balancing against the United States"; T. V. Paul, "Soft Balancing in the Age of U.S. Primacy," *International Security,* Vol. 30, No. 1, Summer 2005, pp. 46-71.

42. "Speech by the Foreign Minister of Brazil, Ambassador Celso Amorim, at the G-33 Ministerial Meeting, Jakarta, March 21, 2007," available from *www.brazil.org.uk/press/speeches_files/20070321.html*; Daniel Flemes, *Emerging Middle Powers' Soft Balancing Strategy: State and Perspectives of the IBSA Dialogue Forum*, Working Paper No. 57, Hamburg, Germany, German Institute of Global and Areas Studies, August 2007, p. 18.

43. "Brazil: Iraq, U.S. Guilty of 'Disrespect,'" *Newsmax Wires,* March 20, 2003.

44. "Lecture by the Foreign Minister of Brazil, Ambassador Celso Amorim, Given at the London School of Economics on March 17, 2004"; also "Speech by the President of Brazil, Luiz Inácio Lula da Silva, at the General Debate of the 64th UN General Assembly, New York, September 23, 2009," available from *www.brazil.org/uk/press/speeches*.

45. For instance, "Cape Town Communiqué," March 11, 2005, available from *www.info.gov.za/speeches/2005/05031408451001.htm*.

46. "Speech by the President of Brazil, Luiz Inácio Lula da Silva, at the Plenary Meeting of the 61st General Assembly; Flemes, *Emerging Middle Powers Soft Balancing Strategy,* p. 12.

47. Geographical imprecision aside, the developing world is often referred to as the "Global South."

48. S. P. Guimarães, *Quinhentos Anos de Periferia* (*Five Hundred Years on the Periphery*), Rio Grande do Sul, Brazil: Editora da Universidad Contraponto, 1999, p. 141; also "India-Brazil-South Africa Dialogue Forum, Sixth Trilateral Commission Meeting Ministerial Communiqué," September 1, 2009, available from *www2.mre.gov.br/ibas/2009_09_01_Brasilia_VI_Comista.pdf*.

49. Malcolm Moore, "China Overtakes the US as Brazil's Largest Trading Partner," *Telegraph,* May 9, 2009; "Brazil, China to Postpone Joint Satellite Launching to 2011," *People's Daily Online,* February 11, 2010; John Lyons, "Brazil Turns to China to Help Finance Oil Projects," *Wall Street Journal,* May 18, 2009.

50. "Iran and Latin America," *Latin American Special Report*, December 2009; Ariel Farrar-Wellman, "Brazil-Iran Foreign Relations," January 26, 2010, available from *IranTracker.org*; "Brazil and Iran: An Unlikely Partnership," *Stratfor*, November 25, 2009.

51. "Amorim destaca protagonismo internacional do Brasil" ("Amorim Emphasizes Brazil's International Protagonism"); "Trade Blocs in Latin America: The State of Play after Cancun," *Latin American Special Report*, July 2004.

52. Rothkopf, "The World's Best Foreign Minister"; "Geopolitical Diary: The Birth of BRIC," *Stratfor*, June 16, 2009.

53. "India-Brazil-South Africa Dialogue Forum, Sixth Trilateral Commission Meeting Ministerial Communiqué."

54. "Brazil, India, S. Africa Demand G-20 to Fulfill Commitments," *Global Times*, September 2, 2009.

55. "IBSA Leaders Agree to Form Coordinating Mechanism to Deal with Global Financial Crisis," *Thai Indian*, October 15, 2008.

56. "IBSA Naval Exercise No Precursor to Treaty," *Thai Indian*, May 13, 2008.

57. "Speech by the Foreign Minister of Brazil, Ambassador Celso Amorim, at the Meeting of the Ministerial Commission of the IBSA Forum, New Delhi, India, July 17, 2007," available from *www.brazil.org.uk/press/speeches_files/20070717.html*.

58. This discussion of region formation is drawn from Thomas Pederson, "Cooperative Hegemony: Power, Ideas and Institutions in Regional Integration," *Review of International Studies*, Vol. 28, No. 4, Fall 2002, pp, 677-696; Daniel Flemes and Thorsten Wojczekwsi, "Contested Leadership in International Relations: Power Politics in South America, South Asia and Sub-Saharan Africa," Paper No. 121, Hamburg, Germany: German Institute of Global and Area Studies, February 2010. For a variation on this idea, see Andres Rivarola Puntigliano, "Global Shift: The U.N. System and the New Regionalism in Latin America," *Latin American Politics and Society*, Vol. 49, No. 1, Spring 2007, pp. 89-112.

59. "'Assertive' bid to change power balance"; Jens Glusing, "Brazil Flexes Muscles over Honduras Crisis," *Der Spiegel Online,* October 9, 2009. See also "Entrevista Ministro das Relações Exteriores, Embaixador Celso Amorim, ao jornalista Boris Casoy, no Programa Passando a Limpo" ("Interview given by the Minister of Foreign Relations, Ambassador Celso Amorim, to the journalist Boris Casoy, on the program *Passando a Limpo*"), October 4, 2003, available from *www.mre.gov.br/portugues/politica_externa/discursos/discurso_detalhe3.asp?ID_DISCURSO=2214.*

60. Brazilian concerns are discussed in Sara Miller Llana, "Brazil, Venezuela Vie for Energy Clout," *Christian Science Monitor,* August 10, 2007; "Gas Has Become the Pivot of Brazil's Moves to Neutralize Hugo Chávez," *Latin American Security & Strategic Review,* May 2006; Sean Burges, "Building a Global Southern Coalition: The Competing Approaches of Brazil's Lula and Venezuela's Chávez," *Third World Quarterly,* Vol. 28, No. 7, October 2007, pp. 1343-1352.

61. Sean Burges, "Consensual Hegemony: Theorizing Brazilian Foreign Policy after the Cold War," *International Relations,* Vol. 22, No. 1, April 2008, p. 78; "Arms Transfers as Instruments of Foreign Policy," *Latin American Security & Strategic Review,* October 2009; "'Assertive' Bid to Change Power Balance."

62. Burges, "Consensual Hegemony," pp. 65-84.

63. "Brazil's Foreign Policy under Lula," *Latin American Special Report,* May 2004. This idea goes back several administrations prior to Lula's, although his has advanced it most diligently. See Rubens Antonio Barbosa, "O Lugar do Brasil no Mundo" ("Brazil's Place in the World"), *Política Exterior,* Vol. 5, No. 2, September 1998, pp. 69-82.

64. María Regina Soares de Lima and Mónica Hirst, "Brazil as an Intermediate State and Regional Power: Action, Choice, and Responsibilities," *International Affairs,* Vol. 82, No. 1, January 2006, p. 34; "Brazil's Foreign Policy under Lula"; J. F. Hornbeck, *Mercosur: Evolution and Implications for U.S. Trade Policy,* Washington, DC: Congressional Research Service, August 23, 2006, pp. 1-5; "Mercosur Agrees on Concessions to Paraguay, Uruguay, as Chávez Casts Cloud over Summit," *Bridges Weekly Trade News Digest,* July 11, 2007.

65. Burges, "Consensual Hegemony," pp. 76-77; Flemes and Wojczewski, "Contested Leadership in International Relations," p. 12.

66. "Mercosur Defense Chiefs Disagree with U.S. on Obsolescence of Conventional Forces," *Latin American Security & Strategic Review,* September 2004.

67. "Reviving the Idea of a Subregional Defense Council," *Latin American Security & Strategic Review,* March 2008.

68. "Mr. Luiz Inácio Lula da Silva, President of the Federal Republic of Brazil," Address to the Council on Foreign Relations.

69. Shannon quoted in "Brazil, Buoyed by Oil and Agriculture, Becomes a Global Power," *Latin America News,* September 19, 2008; Sarkozy quoted in "France's Sarkozy in Brazil," *Latin American Regional Review: Brazil & Southern Cone,* January 2009.

70. Nilson Brandão Junior and Marianna Aragão, "Miséria no Brasil Cai 27,7% no 1° Mandato de Lula" ("Poverty in Brazil Falls 27.7% in Lula's First Term"), *O Estado de Sao Paulo,* September 20, 2007; "Brazil: Half the Nation, a Hundred Million Citizens Strong," *Economist,* September 13, 2008, pp. 43-44.

71. World Bank, "Brazil at a Glance," September 24, 2008, available from *devdata.worldbank.org/AAG/bra_aag.pdf.*

72. Puroshothaman, "Dreaming with BRICs," p. 12.

73. World Bank Group, "Featured Snapshot Report," 2009, available from *www.enterprisesurveys.org/ExploreEconomies/?econ omyid=28&year=2009*; PBS NewsHour, "Brazil's Economic Boom Marred by Social Inequalities," June 9, 2008, available from *www. pbs.org/newshour/bb/latin_america/jan-june08/brazil_06-09.html*; Thomas Kenyon and Emerson Kapaz, "The Informality Trap: Tax Evasion, Finance, and Productivity in Brazil," *Public Policy for the Private Sector,* Note No. 301, World Bank, December 2005, pp. 1-3.

74. Sotero and Armijo, "To Be or Not to Be a BRIC," pp. 66-68; World Bank, "Brazil Country Brief"; Irineu Evangelista de Carv-

alho Filho, "Household Income as a Determinant of Child Labor and School Enrollment in Brazil: Evidence from a Social Security Reform," IMF Working Paper WP/08/241, Washington, DC: International Monetary Fund, 2008, p. 5.

75. Paulo Prada and Kenneth Rapoza, "Stuck at the Crossroads: A Wobbly Road Network and Weak Railways Could Kill Brazil's Export Book," *Latin Trade,* October 2004, available from *findarticles.com/p/articles/mi_m0BEK/is_10_12/ai_n7579928/pg_5/?tag=content;col1.*

76. On these issues, see Peter Meyer and Clare Ribando Seelke, *Brazil-U.S. Relations,* Washington, DC: Congressional Research Service, August 18, 2009, pp. 4-6; "Another Political Reform Project Bites the Dust," *Latin American Regional Report: Brazil & Southern Cone,* June 2009; "Oil: Brazil's Second Independence."

77. "Brazil," available from *Doing Business 2010, www.doingbusiness.org.*

78. The relationship between stronger growth and poverty reduction is discussed in Francisco H. G. Ferreira, Phillippe G. Leite, and Martin Ravallion, "Poverty Reduction without Economic Growth? Explaining Brazil's Poverty Dynamics, 1985-2004," Policy Research Working Paper No. 4431, Washington, DC: World Bank, December 2007. On Serra, see "Lula's Optimistic Claims for UNASUR," *Latin American Regional Report: Brazil & Southern Cone,* September 2009.

79. Stephanie Hanson, "Brazil's Powerful Prison Gang," Council on Foreign Relations Backgrounder, September 26, 2006, available from *www.cfr.org/publication/11542/;* Samuel Logan, "Riots Reveal Organized Crime Power in Brazil," *International Relations and Security Network,* May 18, 2006; William Langewiesche, "City of Fear," *Vanity Fair,* April 2007, available from *www.vanityfair.com/politics/features/2007/04/langewiesche200704.*

80. Rafael Bielsa quoted in "Strategic Realignment Redefined," *Latin American Security & Strategic Review,* May 2005. A number of non-Latin American countries, including the United States, Russia, and China, have also been cool to Brazil's Security Council bid.

81. See Pederson, "Cooperative Hegemony"; Flemes and Wojczekwsi, "Contested Leadership in International Relations." During the Cold War, for instance, the United States constructed an "empire by invitation" by providing military protection to its European allies and overseeing a relatively open economic system. See Geir Lundestad, "Empire by Invitation? The United States and Western Europe, 1945-1952," *Journal of Peace Research,* Vol. 23, No. 3, September 1986, pp. 263-277.

82. On these issues, consult "La renegociación sobre Itaipú se reanuda hoy" ("Renegotiation on Itaipú Resumes Today"), *ABC Digital,* January 31, 2010; Burges, "Consensual Hegemony," pp. 78-79; Joshua Goodman, "Brazil: The Global Power Looking for a Backyard," *SAIS Review,* Vol. 29, No. 2, Summer-Fall 2009, pp. 7-9; "Fundación para las Relaciones Internacionales y el Diálogo" ("Foundation for International Relations and Dialogue"); "IBSA: An International Actor and Partner for the EU?" Working Paper 63, July 2008, p. 12.

83. The phrase "original sin" is used in G. Calfat, R. G. Flores, M. F. Granato, and A. Rivas, "Dealing with MERCOSUR Asymmetries: Criteria for Allocating Regional Fund Resources," Washington, DC: InterAmerican Development Bank, September 30, 2009, p. 2.

84. *Ibid.,* p. 30; also, "Mercosur Summit Fails to Advance in Internal Trade Issues," *MercoPress,* December 9, 2009; Ministerio de Hacienda, "¿Qué es Focem?" ("What is Focem?"), available from *www.hacienda.gov.py/sseei/index.php?c=268.*

85. "La renegociación sobre Itaipú se reanuda hoy" ("Renegotiation on Itaipú Resumes Today"); "Mercosur Reform," *Latin American Regional Report: Brazil & Southern Cone,* June 2009.

86. "Mercosur Summit Fails to Advance in Internal Trade Issues," *MercoPress,* December 9, 2009; Roberto Bouzas, "The Politics and Economics of Mercosur: Old Challenges, New Approaches," University of Miami, Center for Hemispheric Policy, March 19, 2008, pp. 2-4; Hornbeck, *Mercosur,* pp. 5-7.

87. "Brazil Finds a Role for the Mercosur," *Latin American Regional Report: Brazil & Southern Cone,* August 2009.

88. Burges, "Consensual Hegemony," p. 75.

89. "Brazil Finds a Role for the Mercosur."

90. "Brasil prepara simulacro de guerra dirigido al Paraguay" ("Brazil Prepares Wargame Directed at Paraguay").

91. "Brazil and Chile Lead Strategies to Contain Chávez without Isolating Him," *Latin American Security & Strategic Review,* September 2007; "Arco del Pacífico abrirá el comercio" ("Pacific Arc will unlock commerce'), *El Comercio,* September 11, 2007.

92. "Uruguay: Pese a la oposición interna, Vázquez firma el Tifa" ("Uruguay: Despite Internal Opposition, Vázquez Signs the TIFA"), *Informe Latinoamericano,* February 2, 2007.

93. Oleg Shchedrov, "Russia's Medvedev in Brazil, Aims to Double Trade," *Reuters,* November 25, 2008.

94. "Brazil Recognizes China's Full-Market Economy Status," *People's Daily Online,* November 14, 2004.

95. "The Birth of BRIC," *Stratfor,* June 16, 2009.

96. Sebastian Mallaby, "Brazil's China Headache," *Washington Post,* December 14, 2009; Seth Kugel, "China-Brazil Economic Alliance May Be Exaggerated," *Global Post,* May 27, 2009; China Brief, "The Panda Hugs the Tucano: China's Relations with Brazil," Jamestown Foundation, May 15, 2009.

97. "China's Creeping Expansion Poses Threat to Russia's Far East," *Stratfor,* February 28, 2001; Andrei Piontkovsky, "China's Threat to Russia," *Guardian,* August 27, 2007.

98. Vikas Bajaj, "India Worries as China Builds Ports in South Asia," *New York Times,* February 15, 2010; "Round 2: China and India Back in for Ghana's Oil," *China Africa News,* July 2009.

99. See Ruchita Beri and Prasanta Kumar Pradhan, "IBSA Dialogue Forum: Problems and Prospects," New Delhi, India: Institute for Defense Studies and Analyses, October 15, 2008, available from *www.idsa.in.*

100. Lakshmi Puri, "IBSA: An Emerging Trinity in the New Geography of International Trade," United Nations Conference on Trade and Development, Policy Issues in International Trade and Commodities, Study Series No. 35, 2007, pp. 28-29.

101. "Speech by the Foreign Minister of Brazil, Ambassador Celso Amorim, at the Meeting of the Ministerial Commission of the IBSA Forum, New Delhi, India, July 17, 2007"; Woodrow Wilson International Center for Scholars, "Emerging Powers: India, Brazil and South Africa (IBSA) and the Future of South-South Cooperation," Special Report, August 2009, p, 3; Mario Osava, "IBSA Summit—Will South-South Cooperation Regain Clout?" *IPS News*, September 23, 2008, available from *ipsnews.net/news.asp?idnews=43974.*

102. John Lyons, "Brazil's New Standing Threatened by Ahmadinejad Visit," *Wall Street Journal*, November 23 2009.

103. Hal Brands, *Latin America's Cold War*, Cambridge, MA: Harvard University Press, 2010, chap. 5.

104. Discussed and quoted in *Ibid.*; also Matias Spektor, *Kissinger e o Brasil* ("Kissinger and Brazil"), Rio de Janeiro, Brazil: Zahar, 2009.

105. Monte Reel, "U.S. Seeks Partnership with Brazil on Ethanol," *Washington Post*, February 8, 2007; Christopher McMullen, "U.S.-Brazil Relations: Forging a Strategic Partnership," October 17, 2007, available from *merln.ndu.edu/archivepdf/ARA/State/94355.pdf.*

106. "Lula pede a Obama un novo gesto de abertura em relação a Cuba" ("Lula asks Obama for a New Gesture of Openness in Relation to Cuba"), *O Globo*, April 17, 2009; "OAS Summit Debates Five Proposals on the Cuban Issue," *MercoPress*, June 3, 2009.

107. In early 2009, Obama said of Lula, "I love this guy." See "Obama: Lula is 'Most Popular Politician on Earth,'" *Huffington Post,* April 2, 2009.

108. This point is discussed in Paulo Roberto de Almeida's, "Uma política externa engajada: a diplomacia do governo Lula" ("A committed foreign policy: The diplomacy of the Lula government"), *Revista Brasileira de Política Internacional,* Vol. 47, No. 1, June 2004, pp. 162–84.

109. Ambassador Antonia Patriota, "Brazil-U.S. Relations: The Bilateral, Regional and Global Agendas," Providence, RI: Watson Institute, Brown University, February 15, 2008, available from *www.watsoninstitute.org/events_detail.cfm?id=1064;* "Lula Strikes 'Strategic Alliance' with France," *Latin American Security & Strategic Review,* February 2008.

110. On ethanol and agricultural subsidies, see "Brazil's Lula Presses Obama on Doha," *Bridges Weekly Trade News,* March 18, 2009; "Speech by the President of Brazil, Luiz Inácio Lula da Silva, at the Special Meeting of the UN Economic and Social Council (ECOSOC) on the World Food Crisis, New York, May 20, 2008," available from *www.brazil.org/uk/press/speeches.*

111. Quoted in "'Assertive' Bid to Change Power Balance."

112. "Brazil-U.S. Rows Building over Colombia, Biofuel, Trade: FM," *Agence France Presse,* August 2, 2009; "UNASUR Agrees to Condition Foreign Military Presence," *Latin American Security & Strategic Review,* November 2009.

113. "New Fleet May Mean U.S. Covets Brazil's Oil: Lula," *Reuters,* September 18, 2008.

114. "Brazilian Faults Obama's Handling of Honduran Coup," *Latin American Herald Tribune,* October 21, 2009; "Brasil espera una actitud más firme de EEUU contre el golpe" ("Brazil Expects a Firmer U.S. Attitude Against the Coup"), *EFE News Service,* August 4, 2009; Glusing, "Brazil Flexes Muscles over Honduras Crisis"; Andre Soliani and Iuri Dantas, "Lula to Mend Honduras Ties as Brazil Seeks More Clout," *Bloomberg News,* February 22, 2010.

115. Engel quoted in Lyons, "Brazil's New Standing Threatened by Ahmadinejad Visit"; and "Iran and Latin America."

116. "Clinton Fails to Win over Brazil on Iran," *New York Times,* March 3, 2010.

117. Brian Wampler and Leonardo Avritzer, "The Spread of Participatory Democracy in Brazil: From Radical Democracy to Participatory Good Government," *Journal of Latin American Urban Studies,* Vol. 7, Fall/Winter 2006, pp. 37-52; Joshua Partlow, "To Rid Slums of Drug Gangs, Police in Rio Try War Tactics," *Washington Post,* January 6, 2009; "Brasil: infraestructuras, menos impuestos y bajos intereses, ejes del plan de Lula" ("Brazil: Infrastructure, Less Taxes and Low Interest, Central Ideas of Lula's Plan"), *Infolatam,* January 23, 2007.

118. Eliot Brockner, "Brazil Buys Bolivian Textiles: When the Value of a Dollar is Worth So Much More," *Americas Quarterly Online,* September 2, 2009, available from *www.americasquarterly. org.*

119. This case is made persuasively in Calfat, Flores, Granato, and Rivas, "Dealing with MERCOSUR Asymmetries," pp. 30-31.

120. Report by the Trade Advisory Group, "Building the Hemispheric Growth Agenda: A New Framework for Policy," Washington, DC: Americas Society, January 13, 2009, p. 11.

121. See "The Return of the 4th Fleet," *Stratfor,* April 25, 2008.

122. Robert Chase, Emily Hill, and Paul Kennedy, *The Pivotal States: A New Framework for U.S. Policy in the Developing World,* New York: Norton, 1999, p. 194.